America Learns to Dance

America Learns to Dance

A HISTORICAL STUDY OF DANCE EDUCATION IN AMERICA BEFORE 1900

by

JOSEPH E. MARKS III

One of the series of republications by

DANCE HORIZONS   •   NEW YORK

One of a series of republications by Dance Horizons, 1801 East 26th
Street, Brooklyn, N.Y. 11229

This is an unabridged republication of the first edition published by
Exposition Press, New York, in 1957. © 1957 by Joseph E. Marks III.

International Standard Book Number 0-87127-081-1

Library of Congress Catalog Card Number 75-9162

Printed in the United States of America

To

who gave the inspiration

and to

TED SHAWN

who illumined the way

Preface

BOTH DANCE AND EDUCATION are as old as man himself. Both have had their periods of rise and decline and, in some form or other, both have survived their lean years so that we may enjoy them today. Dance, possibly more than education, has had a rough path to follow, being, at various ages during the history of man, sometimes an adjunct to religion or a means of education, as well as a recreation and an art form.

Those men and women who landed on the shores of the New World brought with them customs, ideas, and mores that were a part of the Old World. They based their ideas of education, as well as the many other practices that made up their daily lives, upon what they had done in their homelands. Dance and dance education formed a part of the life of England, France, and Holland at the time of colonization. It was only after the colonists had become somewhat self-sufficient that the many miles of ocean between the continents caused them to lose old habit patterns. Their new country brought forth new problems and required new methods to solve them.

Because the writer believes that the geographic, economic, religious, and cultural conditions are reflected in the education of a people, he has tried to give some background in these various fields and show how it had an influence on the dance education of the day.

The generally accepted historical limits have not been used. Instead, the book has been divided into three periods, each covering a century. The important events in each century have been recorded and, while many of the events continue into the following century, only when there has been a definite change in these events was this change noted. The date of 1900 was chosen as a stopping place because at this point dance had become an integral part of education and much of the dance history after this period has been treated in other works. Certain limitations have been necessary, and therefore the book does not deal with the education or performing of ballet or stage dancing, as these also have been treated in other histories.

The writer does not claim originality. His aim has been to gather the scattered bits of history on dance education in order that they may be in one convenient place. Many of the references will be readily recognized as being used in most of the standard histories; others have been hidden away in church histories, biographies, school catalogues and magazines, and many other places which are less accessible. Therefore the only claim that can be made is that a great amount of reading has been done and many notes taken.

If this book serves as a guide and source book of what in the past was felt to be the place and best use of dance education and, in the light of this knowledge, helps to form a sounder philosophy of dance education for the future, its aim will be fulfilled.

J. E. M.

Acknowledgments

BY THE NATURE of this book I am indebted to many people: to those authors whose works I have referred to often, and to the many friends who have offered helpful suggestions.

I especially want to thank Mrs. Ed Petsch, who read and corrected the manuscript. She also offered many ideas, as did Messrs. T. Wild and James Irvin. Misses Polly Warren, Kate Irvin and Josephine Bull, of the University of Kentucky library, aided in many ways in the gathering of material. Miss Maisie McMichael typed the manuscript. Mrs. Ruth I. Derby helped in untold ways. Special thanks are due to Virginia Butterfield, whose encouragement was a source of help when the spirit was low, and to my mother, Mrs. W. S. Webb.

J. E. M.

Contents

PART ONE

Dance Education in the Seventeenth Century

WHEN the *Mayflower* landed in 1620, the Puritans found a country which had vast natural resources but which presented them with nothing other than what they earned through persistent toil and hardship. They had to work and work hard for everything. They had to clear the land before they could cultivate it; they had to hunt and fish for food; and while their efforts were abundantly rewarded, nevertheless they had little time to spare for recreation.

The Puritans came to the new world in order to set up a society based on a Calvinistic interpretation of the Bible. They believed that they were a chosen people and that by coming to a new land and making their own laws and regulations, they could keep their "Bible religion" pure. The early government of Massachusetts was a theocracy, run by Puritan ministers, who thought the Bible was the disclosed word of God, and that its meaning and intention on every subject had been made plain and explicit to those men with proper learning.[1] This belief not only held for theology but for every phase of life, including dance.

Not all the people who came to New England were Puritans, or even members of the church. Roger Williams preached against this theocracy and was banished from Massachusetts, as Ann Hutchinson had been. In addition there were Quakers, who believed in a more democratic religion. They became an influencing force in the country.

---

[1] Notes appear at the back of the book.

Another blow to the "Bible Commonwealth" was the annulment by England of the old charter and the sending over of a governor to represent the king.

By the end of the seventeenth century, theocracy had been decidedly weakened. Such a form of government was doomed from the first because it went against the natural instinct of the English for liberty. Man's philosophy was also turning toward rationalism and liberalism.[2] While the Puritan church was standing still, the world around it was changing.

The Puritans had realized soon after they landed that some form of education was necessary. They knew that if they were to teach God's word, they must teach the people to read the Bible; therefore, in the very early days, children were taught by the ministers or by their parents. Boston, however, felt a need for further training of its young citizens, and in 1635 established the Boston Latin Grammar School. A year later, Harvard College came into existence, with the training of ministers as its main objective.

All the children did not attend grammar school or college, but they were required by Massachusetts law to have some form of training. They became apprentices in the various trades. In these ways, Massachusetts became a leader in the educational field and was taken as an example by many of the other colonies.

II

Dancing was not in disfavor with the Puritans, as so often has been thought. Percy A. Scholes in his book, *The Puritans and Music in England and New England*,[3] has taken great pains to set the matter straight. Dancing did, however, take on the curse of paganism when associated with feasts or public demonstrations. But where dancing was justified by the Bible, it was not wrong; so long as it was used as the Bible stated it should be used.

In 1625, Reverend John Cotton, while still in England, gave an idea how ministers felt about dancing, but he was more liberal than many. He did not condemn mixed dancing because he could justify it by the Bible. He said:

> Dancing (yea though mixt) I would not simply condem. For I see two sorts of mixt dancings in use with God's people in the Old Testament, the one religious, Exod. XV, 20, 21, the other civil, tending to the praise of conquerors, as the former of God, I Sam. XVII, 6, 7. Only lascivious dancing to wanton ditties, and amorous gestures and wanton dalliances, especially after feasts, I would bear witness against, as a great *flabella libidinis.*[4]

This was the same John Cotton who came to New England in 1633 and later became the most honored New Englander of his day. He was the leading minister of Boston and New England and his pronouncements from "the pulpit soon became the law of the land or practice of the church."[5]

William Bradford also showed his dislike of dancing to "wanton ditties" when he wrote, in 1628, of the people dancing around a Maypole. To the Puritan, a Maypole was "a stynchyng idol" around which heathens worshiped. Therefore, this particular incident, where people danced about the Maypole "like so many fairies," disturbed Mr. Bradford and his friend, John Indecott, exceedingly. They were even more disturbed at the "worse practises" of the dancers in composing "sundry rimes & verses, some tending to lasciviousness," which were "affixed to this idle or idoll May-polle." While Bradford did not like the Maypole, he was more concerned with Morton's "trading of pieces, powder, and shotte to ye Indeans," and how he taught them to use the guns; for many "both Dutch & English have been lately slain by those Indeans, thus furnished. . . ." [6]

Despite the fact that the Puritans disliked the Maypole, the ceremony continued for some time. Judge Samuel Sewall wrote in his diary for May 26, 1687, that the people of Charleston cut down a Maypole "and Now a bigger is set up and a garland upon it." The next day he recorded how Father Walker had "overheard some discourse about the Maypole, and told what manner it was in England to dance about it with music; and that 'twas to be feared such practices would be here." [7]

That there was dancing in seventeenth-century New England is shown by the fact that many of the court cases mention dancing in connection with other offenses. Lawrence Waters' wife and friend insisted on dancing in Cambridge in 1638 and were brought to court and "all of them were admonished to avoyed dancing." [8] In 1651, at the court of New Plymouth, "Samuel Eaton and Goodwife Halle, of the towne of Duxburrow," were "Released with admonition" for mixed dancing. [9] And in 1662, John Clark, a servant, ran away from his master two or three times because he desired more liberty and a place where he "might live merrily and sing & daunce &c." [10] Whereas in 1651, it was "observed that there were many abuses & disorders by dauncinge in ordinaryes, whether mixt or unmixt, upon mariage of some p[er]son," and a law was passed stating that upon no occasion would dancing be allowed in the inns and a five-shilling fine would be placed upon those found guilty. While this law forbids dancing in taverns, it says nothing about dancing elsewhere, so long as it is done in its proper place and at a proper time. [11]

New educational theories in England were soon known to the Puritans in New England, as there was a constant exchange of ideas between the two localities. Many of the ministers, before leaving England, were familiar with the early English educational writers who saw dance as a part of education. Sir Thomas Elyot had included dance in *The Boke named the Governour* in 1531, as did Roger Ascham in *The Scholemaster* (1571), and Mulcaster in his *Positions* (1581). Later, the Puritan poet, John Milton, had mentioned dance in his poetry to show the delights of England. In his *Tractate on Education* (1644) he wrote that some form of physical exercise should be used. John Bunyan, a tinker and arch-Puritan, saw dance forming a part of his heaven in *Pilgrim's Progress* (1678).

John Locke, the English philosopher, in *Some Thoughts Concerning Education* (1690) wrote that children should be taught dance as soon as they are capable of learning it. Locke's book, coming at the end of the century, had little influence on the seventeenth century, but many of his ideas on education were advanced for his time. Later educational writers, as well as writers on dance and manners, often quoted from Locke.

"Dancing," wrote Locke, "being that which gives *graceful Motions* all the Life, and above all things Manliness, and a becoming Confidence to young Children, I think cannot be learned too early. . . ." He warns however, that a good dancing master is necessary; one who knows and can teach what is graceful and becoming, otherwise it is better to have none at all. His main reason for including dancing was "it gives Children manly Thought and Carriage, more than any thing." [12]

Charles Morton, an instructor at Harvard and author of *Compendium Physicae* (1687), a book used by Harvard students, stated that despite the abuse by man's corruption, the gymnastic arts, which included dancing, were invented and taught for the regulating of poise and were therefore of great use.[13]

The book that was to influence the Puritans the most, as far as dance was concerned, was the Puritan publication of the first English dance book in 1651. On March 19th of that year, John Playford published the first edition of *The English Dancing Master: or, Plain and Easie Rules for Dancing of Country Dances, with the Tune to Each Dance.* The book consisted of the simple, native folk dances and was intended to be a reminder for the practicing dancer. The descriptions are in technical form and terms current to dance of that period.[14] The book met with such a popular demand that it ran through seventeen editions between 1651 and 1728.

At the beginning of the book, Playford stated "To the Ingenious Reder" that—

> The Art of Dancing . . . is a commendable and rare Quality fit for yong Gentlemen, if opportunely and civilly used. . . . This art has been Anciently handled . . . and much commend it to be Excellent for Recreation, after more serious studies, making the body active and strong, graceful in deportment, and a quality very much beseeming a Gentleman.[15]

Because dance taught manners and manners were considered a part of morals, the Puritans could justify its use. Playford's dances also were democratic in that they were circle or round dances and, therefore, there was not a head couple, a position which in the dances of the court was reserved for the elite.[16]

The first dancing masters in New England were not of the most reputable character and brought down upon their heads the wrath of the Boston ministers. The first dancing master was said to be in 1672, with no further data available.[17] Then came Henry Sherlot, a Frenchman, who, according to the *Records of the Court of Assistants,* was a "person very Insolent & of ill fame that Raues & scoffes at Religion, of a Turbulent spirit no way fitt to be tolerated to live in this place. . . ."[18] He was ordered not only out of the town but out of the colony. Later, Francis Stepney came to Boston with the purpose of setting up a dancing school for mixed dancing, and he was to hold his classes on Lecture Day, which to Puritan Boston was a day of worship. Judge Sewall wrote of the incident in his diary for Thursday, November 12, 1685, stating that—

> After, the Ministers of this Town Come to the Court and complained against a Dancing Master who seek to set up here and hath mixt Dances, and his time of Meeting is Lecture-Day; and 'tis reported he should say that by one Play he could teach more Divinity than Mr. Willard or the Old Testament. Mr. Moody said 'Twas not time for N. E. to dance. Mr. Mather struck at the Root, speaking against mixt Dances.[19]

The court, according to Judge Sewall, ordered Stepney not to keep a dancing school: "if he does will be taken in contempt and be proceeded with accordingly." However, the court did fine him 100 pounds for his "Blasphemous words and Reviling the Goverment" and, to show even a greater lack of character, Stepney ran away from his debt.[20]

The Stepney incident was not taken lightly by the ministers of Boston. To show where they stood on the matter of mixed dancing, they wrote a tract entitled, *An Arrow*

Against Profane and Promiscuous Dancing, drawn out of the quiver of the Scriptures. By the Ministers of Christ at Boston in New-England. Increase Mather, father of Cotton Mather, is believed to have written the tract, and at the very beginning of it he stated that—

> Concerning the Controversy about *Dancing*, the question is not whether all *Dancing* be in itself sinful. It is granted, that *Pyrrhical* or *Polemical Saltation:* i.e. where men vault in their Armour, to shew their strength and activity, may be of use. Nor is the question, whether a sober and grave *Dancing* of Men with Men, or of Women with Women, be not allowable; we make no doubt of that, where it may be done without offence, in due season, and with moderation. The Prince of Philosophers has observed truly, that *Dancing* or *Leaping* is a natural expression of joy: so that there is no more Sin in it, than in laughter, or any outward expression of inward Rejoycing.[21]

The question that concerned the ministers was whether or not "*Gynecansrical Dancing*, or that which is commonly called *Mixt* or *Promiscuous Dancing*, viz. of Men and Women," was lawful and could be indulged in without sin. Quoting from Augustine, Chrysostom, Ambrose and many others, the ministers proved to themselves, and they hoped to everyone else, that mixed dancing was sinful and therefore unlawful. Their main reason for condemning mixed dancing was that it was an incentive to break the Seventh Commandment, which states, "Thou shalt not commit adultery." [22]

Although believing that mixed dancing was sinful and should not be indulged in, the ministers were not against dance schools or dance teachers. To Plea 2 of Argument 6 of *An Arrow*, that "*The Design of Dancing is only to teach Children good Behavior and decent Carriage*," the ministers answered that "Religion is no Enemy to good Manners," and to "learn a due Poyse and Composure of Body is not unlawful. But, if any parent is desirous in having his children learn what may be truly ornamental or a desirable accomplishment, let them send their children to a grave person who will teach them decency of behaviour, and each sex by themselves." [23]

Despite the ministers' statement against mixed dancing, the people of New England continued the practice, and, by 1700, the "People of Quality" began to give balls.

Such a practice disturbed Cotton Mather. In *A Cloud of Witnesses*, he let it be known to all that he did not approve of balls or mixed dancing. Like his father, he did not find it wrong for parents to send their children to a dancing master where they might learn to carry themselves handsomely in company. The question that bothered Cotton Mather was whether balls, which "lead the Young People of both Sexes unto great Liberties with each other," are not a "Vanity" which is forbidden by Christianity.[24]

To prove that balls and mixed dancing were not approved by the "Rules of Christianity," Mather followed the footsteps of his father in quoting the "Authorities." Mather also had a word to say to those ministers, like Timothy Edwards, who had an Ordination Ball and the English Nonconformist ministers who did not speak against the Boston balls. He reminded the ministers that, according to the old Councils, it was a crime for a minister to be even a spectator at a dance.[25]

Although the Mathers cried against mixed dancing, it became a part of the social life of New England by the end of the seventeenth century. The ministers had sanctioned dancing schools that were run by "Grave Persons" who taught the children "Decency of Behaviour" and how to "carry themselves handsomely." They had seen no harm in the country dances from Playford's *Dancing-Master*, which, to the ministers, were not mixed and taught manners. As for the "People of Quality" who had acquired a certain amount of wealth and leisure, it was only natural for them to have balls where they might show their gains. The ministers, themselves, had given ordination balls.

The Dutch in New Netherlands had danced in Holland at *kermis*, Christmas, and Pinkster. This custom they brought with them to their new homeland. In 1641, Governor Kieft established fairs to encourage the agricultural pursuits of the people. At these fairs dance added to the pleasure of business.[26]

The Dutch had much of their entertainment in the home. The men also had "clubs" that would meet at the taverns, and while the men enjoyed their friends, the children could be seen dancing indoors or on the greens.[27]

Whether or not word of Francis Stepney reached New York before him is not known. However, when he entered the town in 1687, the governor's council forbade him to teach and also ordered him out of the province, unless he could show that he would not become a public charge. Stepney, feeling that he was unjustly banned, sent a petition to the council which granted him permission to appeal to the king in person.[28]

IV

The status of dancing in the southern colonies during the seventeenth century differed from that in New England because of the South's different geographic, economic, and social conditions. The wealthy or ruling class felt that dance was a necessary part of the education of a gentleman, while the servant and slave class saw it as a good form of recreation.

When the London Company landed in 1607 in what was later to be known as Jamestown, Virginia, they found flat land and rolling hills and a long growing season which was suitable for vast cultivation. Tobacco became the basic crop, and the easily navigable bays and streams of the coast facilitated the transportation of this export to England and other parts of the world. Because of the cultivation of such vast acreage, great plantations arose which caused the need for servants and slaves to tend such areas and also brought considerable wealth to the owners.

Where the people of New England had come to the new world for freedom of religion, the people of Virginia came for economic reasons, for the wealth they could wring from the new, rich soil. There was little religious basis for their social organization, and the church in the South had therefore little influence on civil affairs.

For one thing there was little town life in the South. People lived on farms and plantations that were many miles apart, and this fact made it difficult for them to get to church, even when the weather was favorable. The ministers themselves, of whom there were too few, were unable to get to a church more than once a month, and so they were unable to keep in close touch with their church members. Where the government of New England was theocratic, Virginia's was aristocratic, even oligarchic.[29]

The educational pursuits of Virginia, like the rest of her social, economic, and political organization, followed closely those of England. The London Company tried to establish a college at Henrico in 1619, but the Indian massacre in 1622 brought the work to a close. The people asked the Company to try once again, but they refused, and it was not until 1693 that the College of William and Mary was opened.[30]

The first educational law to be passed was the Apprenticeship Law of 1643 which followed closely the Apprenticeship Law of England. The law had been enacted to take care of the orphans that had been sent over from England.[31] There were a few community schools where various families went together to hire a teacher. The wealthy planter engaged a tutor to care for his children's educational needs, while others sent their sons to colleges in England.

Like New England, Virginia had laws against dancing on the Sabbath. While the offenders never went unpunished, dancing on a Sunday was not a great rarity. In Princess Anne County, in 1691–92, Peter Crashly and his wife, and Thomas Dodds were brought to court for fiddling and dancing on the Sabbath, as was William Johnson of Accomac in 1698.[32]

In the last decade of the century, Margaret Teakle, daughter of the Reverend Mr. Teakle, gave a dance that caused a great scandal. Elizabeth Parker had talked Margaret into giving a dance on a Saturday night while her father was absent. The enjoyment of the company had been so great that the dance lasted through the night till eleven o'clock the next day. When Mr. Teakle returned and found that the house had been desecrated on the Sabbath by dancing, even at the very hour that services were being held, it was too much for the liberal clergyman, and, at the next meeting of court, Elizabeth Parker and her husband were charged.[33]

Virginia held very closely to her associations with the mother country and eagerly followed the changes of custom and fashion in England, news of which was brought by boat. Their social classes were built on the English system and the large plantation owners followed closely the life of the English country squires. This held true for their indoor diversions of which dance formed an important part.[34]

The Virginia planter was known for his hospitality. Because he was at such a distance from his neighbor, the Virginia planter made a real occasion of the visit of any of his friends. These visits usually called for a party, which lasted several days. At such times dancing would fill many of the hours, the music for which was performed by some female member of the family, or sometimes by slaves or servants who played the fiddle or called the dances.[35]

Durand, a Hugenot exiled in Virginia for his religion, tells of such a party given by Colonel Fitzhugh. Fitzhugh not only treated the guests royally by providing them with beds and good wine, he also "sent for three fiddlers, a jester, a tight-rope dancer, an acrobat who tumbled around, & they gave us all the entertainment one could wish for." [36]

With dance playing a conspicuous role in the social life of the Virginia planter, it was not long before the dancing master was in demand and, by the end of the century, Virginia was well supplied with dancing masters. Charles Cheat, and his servant, Clason Wheeler, who accompanied him on the fiddle, was one of the dancing masters who taught in the colony. Later, they were to be found in New England, where they had fled for safety, after their side had lost in the Insurrection of 1676.[37]

Dance served an even more important role than that of social amusement. It was believed to be one of the accomplishments proper for a gentleman, and not having a knowledge of dance showed a lack of the proper education. Writers on aristocratic education expected a gentleman to

dance well but not to become so proficient that he rival the
dancing master.

In the library of the Virginia planter were those books
that dealt with the education of a gentleman. One of these
books was Richard Brathwaite's *The English Gentleman*
which includes, as one part of a gentleman's education, the
"Recreation." Under this heading are dancing and fencing,
which are "Ornaments to grace and accomplish them."
Dancing was learned chiefly to "grace and beautifie them!"
although he warns that—

> . . . in neither of these would I have them imitate their
> masters. . . . Or in their *Dancing* those mimicke trickes which
> our apish professants use; but with a reserved grace to come
> off bravely and sprightly, rather than with an affected curi-
> osity. . . . For in exercises of this kinde (sure I am) those
> only deserve most commendation, which are performed with
> least affectation." [38]

Brathwaite also had something to say about the education of the English gentlewoman. The gentlewoman must
not prefer the dance above her religious tasks. However,
"To lead a dance gracefully; . . ." was a commendable
quality.[39]

"*Dancing* is not of itself a Fault," wrote the Lord Marquess of Halifax, in *Advice to a Daughter* (1688), "but
remember that the end of your Learning it, was that you
might better know how to move *gracefully*." Like the gentleman, the lady was warned that if one goes beyond the point
of just learning to be graceful she would be "excelling in a
Mistake, which is no Commendation." Instead she should
dance "Carelessly, like a diversion, rather than with Sol-
emnity as if it was a business." [40]

V

The court dances in favor during the seventeenth century were the pavan, allemande, courante, sarabande, galliard, passepied and minuet. Of all the dances of the period, the minuet lasted the longest and best reflected the life and state of society of the lady and gentleman.

The minuet was introduced into England at the court of Charles II but did not reach the height of fashion till the end of the century. It went through many changes, each making it more rigid, more stately, but less difficult to dance, as the ornamental steps were gradually dropped and a set pattern was adopted. With its graceful bows, its neat and precise steps, the stately carriage of the body, arms and head, it gave both the dance and dancer the dignity that was so much esteemed by aristocratic society.

The minuet was not the type of dance that could be learned by watching. It required a dancing master's knowledge to see that the music was closely followed; the feet and knees were well turned out; the steps were neat and precise; and the gestures of head, arms, hands and body followed closely to the steps and movements of the legs and feet. Strict decorum was followed in removing and replacing the hat and in asking a lady to dance. All this was to be executed with a natural dignity and without affectation.

It therefore was the task of the seventeenth-century dancing master to see that his students not only learned the dances of the day, but also performed them with ease and grace; that they walked with proper carriage and dignity; and followed the deportment that had been set up by the best of society and educational writers of the century.

PART TWO

Dance Education in the Eighteenth Century

AT THE BEGINNING of the eighteenth century, many of the
hardships of founding a new country had been surmounted.
In the eighty years since the *Mayflower* landed, the trees
had been cut; small farms had been started; merchant ships
had been built and were now traveling the seas with their
loads of goods. Most of the towns were situated on the
coast or on navigable rivers and each carried on its own
commerce with the mother country. Communication between the towns themselves was more or less difficult, as
there were few roads, and each town was therefore a unit
within itself. English was slowly becoming the predominant
language throughout the Dutch and German colonies; and
Puritanism, in spite of the ground it had lost, still exerted
some influence over the rules of both church and state.

As the century progressed, more and more people began
to migrate to the new country. As the small towns became
more inhabited, some of the people began to feel crowded
and pushed further up the streams, while others extended
the frontier line to the mountains. Still feeling cramped,
they continued to forge westward till the mountains were
crossed and the western boundary was marked by the Mississippi. "The grand division of the United States is into two
parts," observed *The Monthly Magazine and American
Review* for January, 1800. "The first is that which lies on the
Atlantic Ocean and among those streams that flow into it.
The second is the region adjacent to the lakes and Mississippi." The country was now divided into the "Eastern or

Atlantic portion" and "the western portion . . . which is bordered by the northern lakes, westward by the Mississippi and southward by the Gulph of Mexico." [1]

Communication between the towns had improved somewhat, but at best it was slow and uncertain. Goods were shipped by boat down the rivers at scheduled times "with wind and weather permitting." Land travel was by horseback or stage and, if the trip was of considerable distance, it meant several stops along the way at the inns or taverns which were not the most comfortable.

New England still led the way in its provision for public-supported schools. Outside New England the people still thought that education was the duty of the family or church. The south still followed the English system and left the education of the children to the parents who could afford it, while the poorer children were partially taken care of through apprenticeships or on a charity basis. Colleges and universities were mainly supported and maintained by religious denominations. A great number of private teachers advertised that they intended to open their schools if the public so favored them. They gave instruction in a variety of subjects and at hours which best suited those who desired their help. It is by the curriculum of the private school that the popular educational demands of the day may best be judged. [2] The growing number of newspapers and books became an important instrument in the popular education of the people and supplemented the schools and colleges.

The state of society during the eighteenth century was in constant change. Where religion had played a large role, either directly or indirectly, in the lives of men, it was now losing some of its force. These men began turning their attention to politics and economics. As they commenced to gain some wealth through land holdings, the buying and selling of slaves and, in the north, the rise of commerce, they began to look for outward signs to show their gains. While there had always been some class distinction in America, it now became more evident, since those with greater wealth began to build better houses with finer furnishings. The greatest outward sign was in the rich clothing they wore, for as they went abroad it cried forth to all the position and income of the wearer.

Those who had gained some wealth and position began to have more leisure time for cultural pursuits and amusements. The theatre began to create some interest in the north after 1750. In the south, its influence was seen at an earlier date when William Livingston erected the first playhouse, in Williamsburg, in 1716.[3] In 1735, in the courtroom at Charleston was presented "the Opera of FLORA or *Hob in the Well*, with the Dance of the two Pierrots," and by 1737 a theatre had been erected in Queenstreet.[4]

Music fared somewhat better than did painting, but again the middle and southern colonies were the ones to support the music societies and clubs. While the intellectually elite and rich were interested in science and the arts, the greater mass of men's mental life was taken up with politics and religion.[5]

Just as men's minds had been turned from the old doctrines of religion in their pursuit of greater economic opportunities, there came a series of religious revivals that changed every phase of colonial life. Theodore J. Frelinghuysen had prepared the way as he preached among the Dutch Reformed churches in New Jersey. From there the revival spirit spread to the German communities and reached its height in 1726. In New England, Jonathan Edwards, preaching at Northampton, started the Great New England Awakening in the fall of 1734. Both Frelinghuysen and Edwards prepared the way for George Whitefield, who traveled north and south, and as he preached converted the masses from the worldly habits that they had recently acquired.[6] Whitefield's Great Awakening had largely spent its force by 1744.

Throughout the century there was still the denouncement of dancing by some of the ministers and older members of society. Cotton Mather wrote in *Magnalia Christi Americana* that in New England there were "heinous branches of the seventh commandment" and such things as mixed dancing and light behaviour, which were temptations to break the commandment, had become too common.[7] The young people of Boston caused him much anxiety when they celebrated Christmas with a "Frolick, a revelling Feast and Ball." As many of them belonged to his "Flock," he felt it was his duty if further corruptions were to be prevented, to "bring them under Repentance and prevent such follies for the time to come."[8]

Members of the older generation became aroused at what the younger generation was learning at Mr. Pelham's Dancing School. One of its members complained to the editor of the *Boston News Letter* that as he passed the town house a piece of paper was slipped into his hand which gave "notice of an Entertainment of Music and Dancing, . . . to be held at Mr. Pelham's Dancing School on the Thursday following. . . ." He was greatly startled and concerned that such "Licentious and Expensive diversion [as] music, Balls and Assemblies . . . are hastening the ruin of our country, and are evils which call loudly for a Remedy."[9]

In Philadelphia, in 1706, the Society of Friends (Quakers) at their monthly meeting agreed that "Friends are generally grieved that a dancing & fencing school, are tolerated in this place, which they fear will tend to the corruption of their children." In hopes of stopping the practice they sent a committee to the Governor with a petition condemning dancing and fencing.[10] Again at their Yearly Meeting in 1716, they advised Friends against "going to or being in any way concerned in plays, games, lotteries, music, and dancing." Although the Friends warned the people of Philadelphia against dancing, by the end of the eighteenth century dancing and dancing schools had become a part of its society.

Osiris, a pseudonymous correspondent, grieved when he observed the great demand for dancing schools where young girls were sent before learning to read and write. Writing to the *Philadelphia Minerva,* in 1796, he stated that "dancing was calculated to eradicate solid thought. . . . In fact, versatility of mind, hatred for study, or sober reflection, are the inseparable companions of dancing schools, and the miseries resulting from them are virtually incalculable." [11]

Amelia, another correspondent replying to Osiris' letter in the next issue, suspected him of being a "stiff-jointed rustic, or college recluse" who, as usual, entertains " 'a chaos of fluttering ideas' about the female sex." While she did not advocate ignorance in the female sex, and thought reprehensible indeed the woman who devoted her whole time to dancing, she still believed that:

Whatever captious cynics, in the delirium of their spleen, may allege to the contrary, dancing is incontestably an elegant and amiable accomplishment; it confers grace and dignity of carriage upon the female sex . . . it invigorates the constitution, enlivens the role of the cheek, and in its results operates as silent eloquence upon the hearts of men. Nature gives us limbs, and art teaches us to use them.[12]

Realizing the times, when there was much abuse in all phases of life, and that the morals of men were at a low ebb, Amelia wrote, "It is probably the abuse of dancing which has stimulated Mr. Osiris's ire. . . ." [13] Amelia's statement on dance followed closely that of others who believed that dance had much to offer the young lady and gentlemen.

Like Osiris, the Reverend Devereux Jarratt, minister of Bath Parish, Dinwiddie County, Virginia, felt that dance was wicked. Writing, in 1794, how in his childhood he had been led into the "practices of the ungodly" by copying the examples of his elders, he said: "I was directly led into all *these,* and encouraged therein. *Cards, racing, dancing,* &c. which are still the favorite sport and diversion of the wicked and ungodly were then much in vogue." [14] Across the mountains, in Kentucky, the Bryan Station Baptist Church, in August, 1795, excluded Elizabeth Smith from membership in the church for permitting dancing in her house, although they did not find it inconsistent with the gospel of Christ for her to carry on a distillery of spirits. [15]

The early French in the Illinois country and other points on the upper and lower Mississippi had no worry as to what the older generation or priest would say. For as the young in spirit were active in the dance, the priest and aged patriarch watched smiling as they "lent a sanction and a blessing upon the innocent amusements and useful recreations." [16]

All religions did not discountenance dance. The Shakers, coming to this country from England during the early years of the Revolutionary War, had definite dance patterns as a part of their worship. At first they were largely involuntary and only an outward sign of a highly charged emotion. Like many of the sinners of the early revivals, when they received the "gift" they began to jerk, shake their hands, and dance. In 1788, "the square-order shuffle," the first distinct dance, was introduced into the Shaker worship by Father Joseph, who was opposed to such involuntary emotions, believing that they were a waste of power and purposeless. So in solemn worship the Shakers danced with ". . . a forward and backward movement of ranks, the brethren and sisters in separate groups shuffling towards and away from each other, three paces each way, with a double step or 'tip-tap' at the turn."[17]

The eighteenth century was not without its laws regulating dance. The preceding century had made laws stating where, when, and how people should dance, but because they became ineffective, new laws were made. The Province of Massachusetts Bay published a law in 1712 stating, "that no singing, fiddling, piping, or any other musick, dancing or revelling . . ." would be allowed in any of the taverns or public licensed houses, and if there were offenders, both the offender and tavern keeper would be fined.[18] In the same year, there had been so much trouble with the people making a disturbance at night, causing some of the inhabitants "disrest," that a law was passed forbidding anyone, either by himself or in company with others, to sing, dance, pipe ". . . in any of the streets . . . within any town, in the nighttime. . . ." Offenders would be punished by "sitting in the stocks or cage."[19]

Eighteenth-century New England still observed the Black Sabbath, which began on Saturday evening and lasted for the next twenty-four hours. Several laws had been made to make effective its observance; but because there had been a laxity about its enforcement, the province repealed existing laws and wrote a new one in 1760, in hopes of making more effective the due observance of the Lord's Day. According to the law, one of the things a person was not allowed to do on the Black Sabbath was to "be present at any consert of musick, dancing, or other public diversion." [20]

Later in the century, as the colonies began to seek their independence, the Continental Congress in 1774 resolved to discountenance and discourage "every species of extravagance and dissipation . . . exhibition of shews, plays, and other expensive diversions and entertainments . . ." [21] in hopes of encouraging frugality and economy. Even after the Congress renewed their request that there be no dancing, the French Minister could report to his government that a ball was given by the governor of Philadelphia the day after the resolve was published. [22]

In North Carolina, the Wilmington Committee of Safety resolved "that Balls and Dancing at Public Houses are contrary to the Resolves of the General Congress," and a few days later issued a general warning, declaring as its opinion "that all persons concerned in any dance for the future should be properly stigmatised." Mrs. Auston of Wilmington had made plans for a ball at her house, but was warned by the Committee of Safety to withdraw her plans. Miss Schaw wrote in her journal that she had an invitation to a ball at Wilmington but that "this is the last that is to be given, as the congress has forbid every kind of diversion, even cardplaying." [23]

The attitude of many toward "frivolous" amusements was well summed up in an advertisement in the *Boston Gazette,* in 1767. A printer stated that he had published "An Address to Persons of Fashion, concerning frequenting of Plays, Balls, Assemblies, Card-Tables, &c." and he believed that it was "a Pamphlet worthy the serious attention of every Christian, especially at a Time when Vice and Immorality seem to have ascendency over Religion and the Prince of the Power of the Air reigns with almost an uncontrolled Restraint." [24]

II

Although all through the eighteenth century ministers decried dance, although books were written to tell of its evils, and old-timers wrote and spoke of its uselessness and waste of time and money, and although laws were passed against it, people still danced, and those who did not know how wanted to learn. They danced folk or national dances, which were taught by people recently come from the various countries of Europe and which were handed down from generation to generation; and they danced the fashionable dances which were being taught and danced in the schools and at the great balls of England and France.

As the demand grew greater, dancing schools were set up where dance might be taught, and private schools included dancing in their programs. Boys and girls at private secondary schools were free to elect the courses they desired, and it was up to the successful schoolmaster to offer a variety of subjects. Many schools, therefore, stated in their advertisements that, if required, masters of music and dance would be provided. Charles Peal advertised in 1745 that the Kent County School in Chestertown, Maryland, offered Greek, Latin, writing, and arithmetic and other courses and that "Young gentlemen may be instructed in fencing and dancing by very good masters." [25] Thomas Byerley and Josiah Day of the English Grammar School in New York City announced that among such subjects as letter writing, bookkeeping, trigonometry, surveying, etc., "the undertakers will likewise, if required, provide them masters in the polite accomplishments of Music and Dancing." [26]

While some of the private schools for boys offered dance to their pupils; it was to be found more frequently among the subjects studied in private schools for girls. The Rev-

·erend John Eliot, discussing female education in Boston in 1782, wrote, "We don't pretend to teach ye female part of ye town anything more than dancing, or a little music perhaps, (and these accomplishments must necessarily be confined to a very few,) . . ." [27] Abigail Adams, wife of John Adams, in speaking of female education when she was a schoolgirl, stated that: "Female Education, in the best families, went no further than writing and arithmetic; in some few and rare instances, music and dancing." [28]

Both the Reverend John Eliot's and Mrs. Adams' statements are misleading about the situation in education for girls. While public education for girls during the eighteenth century was in general lacking, there were many private schools throughout the colonies which offered any subject for which there was a demand. While dancing and other subjects considered "accomplishments" did not take the place of the traditional curriculum, they did play an important part in the education of girls. [29]

In 1712, George Brownell offered the young ladies of Boston, "Writing, cyphering, Dancing, Treble Violin, Flute, Spinet, &c." [30] In 1738, Peter Pelham taught both "Young Gentlemen and Ladies . . . Dancing, Writing, Reading, . . ." [31] and other subjects. In Williamsburg, Mrs. Neil stated that she was opening a boarding school for young ladies "on the same Plan of the English Schools," and that "The best Masters will attend to teaching Dancing and Writing." [32] Mary Hext advertised in the *South Carolina Gazette*, in 1741, that she had engaged a "well-qualified master in writing, arithmetic, dancing and music," [33] and Mrs. Duneau announced that "proper masters will attend the young ladies for their Dancing, Music and Drawing. . . ." [34] In Kentucky, Jeremiah Moriarty advertised that he would teach dancing, geography and use of the globes in both Lexington and Danville and that "his character and method are well supported." [35]

Not all schools taught the traditional curriculum. Some of them just taught dancing or dancing combined with one or two other subjects, such as music or fencing. These schools played just as important a part in the education of the fashionable young lady and gentleman as did the writing or reading school. Mr. Enstone, organist for King's Chapel in Boston, opened a dancing school in 1716 where dancing was "taught by a true and easier method than has been heretofore." [36] In Salem, Charles Bradshaw taught French and was allowed to teach dancing "so long as he kept good order." [37] On Thursdays and Fridays, the young ladies and gentlemen of Springfield, Massachusetts could learn dancing from Mr. Allen "in the chamber over Doct. Marcus Marble's store." [38]

Mr. Hulet, a dancing master in New York, advertised that although he could not get a room for his dancing school, he "would attend them in their own houses" if his pupils so desired. He finally opened his "Public Dancing School" in 1770 and announced that he taught at three in the afternoon, but would teach in the evening also for those who could not attend at three. He taught the minuet and country dances and opened a private class for those gentlemen "that have not learned the Hornpipe." [39]

Samuel Perpoint advertised in the *Pennsylvania Mercury* in 1728 and again in 1729 that he gave instruction in dancing and small sword. [40] Ten years later Lewis Mulholland advertised that he would give instruction in dancing to the people of Philadelphia. [41] In Reading, Pennsylvania, Professor Hervey announced that he would open a dancing school at Wood's Tavern. [42]

For twenty shillings a week the young ladies of Williamsburg could study with Sarah Hallam, who, having retired from the stage, opened a dancing school, and "she flatters herself that she shall give entire satisfaction" to those parents who send their daughters.[43] The people who had migrated across the mountains to Kentucky were not long without a dancing master, for John Davenport advertised in the *Kentucky Gazette,* in 1788 that he would hold dancing classes at "Capt. Thomas Young's in Lexington." [44] The citizens of Charleston, South Carolina, in 1732, could gain instruction from Mr. Robinson or in 1749 they could take lessons from either Elizabeth Anderson, James Ciliquet, or William Dering.[45] In Georgia, those desiring to learn to dance could study with Timothy Cronin.[46]

Dancing masters, like preachers, doctors, lawyers, peddlers and many other trades and professions during the eighteenth and early nineteenth centuries, traveled from town to town, often advertising ahead that they planned to open a dancing school "if there be sufficient inducement."

Probably the most famous itinerant dancing teacher was George Brownell, who advertised boarding schools in which he taught dancing in Boston in 1712 and 1734, in New York in 1731, in Philadelphia in 1727, 1730 and 1735, and in Charleston, South Carolina, in 1744.[47] His most famous pupil was Benjamin Franklin, who wrote of him in his *Autobiography.* B. Holdrich left with the printer of the *Kentucky Gazette* in 1798, "A subscription paper, disclosing the terms and object of tuition," for his proposed dancing school. His advertisement informed the people of Lexington, Kentucky, that enough pupils must subscribe before he would venture to their city.

THE subscriber (from Philadelphia) begs leave to inform the Ladies and Gentlemen of Lexington, that, if thirty pupils are subscribed for, he will open a school for one or two months—The subscription to be ascertained by the 21st instant—as the teacher is engaged to return to Pittsburgh at a certain time.[48]

It is doubtful that much dancing can be learned in a month. However, he may have intended only to teach the latest dances to those who had some knowledge of dancing.

Philip Vickers Fithian, tutor to the children at Nomine Hall, one of the Carter plantations in Virginia, states in his journal that he dismissed the children from their classes "on account of Mr. Christian's *Dance*, which, as it goes through his Scholars in Rotation happens to be here to-day."[49] George Washington recorded in his ledger that he paid Mr. Christian for the entrance fee of his nieces Patsy Custis and Milly Possey; and on September 12, 1770, he records in his diary that "Mr. Christian and his Scholars came here to Dancing."[50]

During the eighteenth century, many of the dancing masters were slaves or servants and either taught the children of their masters or the master hired the servants out to teach for them. Thomas Hodge advertised that the ship *Salt Spring* had just arrived and among the servants aboard was a dancing master.[51] Jones Irvine warned all persons that the dancing master Stephen Tenoe was his servant "and that all Sum and Sums of Money due for teaching (by him) to dance, is due and payable to me by the subscriber." But if anyone desired to study from Tenoe, they were able to do so, as Irvin had set up schools at Hampton and Yorktown.[52] Thomas Macoum, who "professes Dancing," ran away and took with him a "Negro Fellow, nam'd *Robin*," who evidently played the fiddle.[53]

It was not always necessary for the dancing master to advertise; at times the towns themselves would advertise that a dancing master would meet with encouragement.

Norborn Parish, in Virginia, advertised for a schoolmaster and also thought a dancing master would succeed.[54] In 1793 Harry Toulmin, in his report on Kentucky and Virginia, stated that in regard to teaching in the counties of Mason and Washington, Kentucky, a dancing master would do well, whereas a music professor would not.[55] Six years later, R. Houghton advertised he was opening a dancing school in Washington, Kentucky.[56]

When some interested persons advertised in the *Providence Gazette* in 1763 that very good encouragement would be given to a teacher who came to their town and opened a school for dancing, fencing, and the violin, they little realized the furor that they would cause. One subscriber opposed such a school in Providence. He wrote to the editor stating that those who were interested might as well set up a *"public Stew or Brothel"* also, so strangers would know where to go to be entertained. However, if the advertisers wanted to be of service to the community, they could set up a school that taught the household arts instead of dancing, for a dancing school was nothing more than a place of vice and debauchery.

Coming to the defense of the dancing school, Philander, a correspondent, wrote the following in the *Providence Gazette and Country Journal:*

> I shall not pretend to prove the Necessity or Propriety of a Dancing-School in this Place. . . . In Regard to Dancing, it is an Amusement neither faulty in itself, nor unlawful; and I dare say, the Gentleman that speaks so bitterly against it, knows very little of the matter . . . otherwise he could not look upon Dancing as inconsistent with Modesty, or blame an Art, that can change a Romp into a polite Lady, that can give a genteel, free air, to the most awkward creature imaginable; in short, an Art that is capable of working

Wonders:- . . . That a Dancing-School or Ball should be a Scene of Lewdness, is to me the greatest absurdity in Nature! What effect Dancing may have on the Vulgar, I can't say, but Modesty and Exactness are the peculiar Characteristics of a regular School or Assembly.[57]

The letters to the editor about the dancing school did not stop with one or two. Others were written taking one side or the other, and one tried to be objective and show both points of view.

During the last quarter of the eighteenth century, an even greater number of dancing masters came to the large cities. Many of them followed closely on the heels of the frontiersmen as they pushed westward. A great number of these dance teachers were of the French nobility, who after the French Revolution sought refuge in America where their genteel accomplishments would help them gain a livelihood. As they traveled from city to hamlet, they taught the fashionable dances of their native land. The dancing masters not only taught the minuet, cotillion, rigadoon, country dances, hornpipe steps, reels and jigs, but also they taught the genteel manners and the graces of head and hand and thereby contributed more to the education of the young boys and girls than just a knowledge of the fashionable dances of the day. After a boy or a girl had gained some knowledge of the basic curriculum, they then turned to the dancing master so that he might "finish" their education by teaching them manners, a graceful carriage, and deportment in genteel company.

Dancing formed a very important part of the education of the wealthy class. Charles Carter of the Cleve plantation wrote in his will that he desired his sons to finish their education which consisted of the languages, mathematics, philosophy, dancing and fencing. He desired his daughter to be taken care of with frugality and have instruction in the dance.[58] Fithian tells how Bob Carter of Nomine Hall was "flogged severely for not having given reasonable notice" that he did not have a pair of dancing shoes and could not go to dancing school. Mr. Carter sent for a pair of shoes and the boy was sent immediately to school.[59] Thomas Jefferson, in making a schedule for his daughter for the use of her time, desired that she dance from ten to one, every other day.[60] President Holyoke, of Harvard College, recorded in his diary that he had paid Mr. Turner, a Boston dancing master, for his daughter, Peggy to attend dancing lessons.[61]

It is impossible to overstress the importance that dance played in the education of the planters' children. While in the North, there was less importance given to dance at the beginning of the century, it became most popular by the middle of the century. In a dialogue of 1744, which "may serve for any part of New England," it shows that some of the mothers wished their daughters taught dancing. The fathers, however, were not in favor of such a plan. The wife insists:

> My dear, you will breed this girl a very fool,
> Why don't you send her to dancing-school?
> See how she holds her head and treads her toes,
> Like a meer Bumpkin, when she stands or goes
> Is so shame-fac'd, tho' enter'd in her teens
> That she looks downward, like a sow in beans.
> Prithee, my dear, consider and bestow
> Good breeding on her for a year or two.

The husband believed that young girls should first be schooled in the household arts then she "shall jig her cupper at the dancing school." The wife then points out that their less fortunate neighbors could afford to send their daughter to dancing school, and with such an argument won the debate.[62]

To aid and guide both the parent and child in the proper instruction of a young lady and gentleman there were a number of books of a mentorial nature. These books were often written in the form of letters or sermons describing not only the duties, virtues and vices, but also often the subjects and books that should be studied and read. In studying these instructional books considerable light is thrown on the opsition that dance held, at least in theory if not in actuality, in the education of the young.[63]

In the *Gentleman Instructed* (1704), Neander, a young gentleman, desires Eusibus, an elderly nobleman, to instruct him in the duties of a gentleman. Neander asks Eusibus what is his opinion concerning dancing. Eusibus replies that while dancing gives "a pretty turn to Breeding" and gives a man all that is necessary for a "quaint address" that he may enter company with advantage it should not be placed "among the first rate qualifications of a Gentleman; for in reality they only fit you up for a modish address, and a Female Entertainment."[64]

Benjamin Franklin wrote to his wife that he hoped that his daughter, Sally, would read many times the *Whole Duty of Man* and *The Ladies' Library*. The latter book was "Written by a Lady" and was a compilation of passages taken from seventeenth-century writers. In writing on dance she quoted from Locke, Lord Halifax, and others. But by selecting from so many authors the book becomes inconsistent and at times must have posed quite a problem for Sally Franklin and its other readers. *The Ladies' Library* considered dance as a recreation valuable for its contributions toward health and deportment; but because it was a recreation, it was placed on the "Margin of Virtue." [65]

Lady Pennington felt that a girl should spend the mornings for "Improvements and the afternoons for diversions." She considered balls as a diversion and dance as a healthful exercise" suitable to the taste and gaity of young minds." [66]

John Gregory's *A Father's Legacy to His Daughters* was printed in the colonies many times, and later, passages were quoted in children's readers. Gregory, like others of the period, believed that the greatest attributes of a young lady were modesty, delicacy, piety, and extreme sensibility. He saw dancing as an elegant accomplishment. The main points a girl must attend to while dancing are ease and grace. She should enjoy herself while dancing but never forget the "delicacy" of her sex.[67] Like Gregory, Dr. Fordyce's *Sermons to Young Women* was considered essential in a young lady's library, and oftentimes it was used as required reading in girls' schools.

Dr. Fordyce could not see any reason for condemning a discreet use of dance, for after all, "what is dancing, in the best sense, but the harmony of motion rendered more palpable?" It was his belief that dancing was adapted "to promote health and good humor, a social spirit, and kind of affections between the sexes." While some abused the use of dance he, for one, could look upon it with "sensible satisfaction" when a young lady danced with a modest mien, in a private circle of friends and relations, and precautions were taken to see that it did not "interfere with health, regularity, modest apparel, and prudent expense." [68]

A book published in Philadelphia whose full title is an epitome of the educational writers of the period is entitled *Sentimental Beauties, and Moral Delineations, from the*

Writings of the Celebrated Dr. Blair, and other much Admired Authors: Selected with a View to Refine the Taste, Rectify the Judgment, and Mould the Heart to Virtue. In the same book a good summary of the ideas on ornamental education for women is given.

> Merely-ornamental accomplishments will but indifferently qualify a woman to perform the *duties* of life, though it is highly proper she should possess them, in order to furnish the *amusements* of it. Yet, though the well-bred woman should learn to dance, sing, recite, and draw; the end of a good education is not that they may become singers, dancers, players, or painters; its real object is, to make them good daughters, good wives, good mistresses, good members of society and good christians.[69]

The writers of the instructional books of the time, concerning themselves with the moral and religious nature of the young, and constantly stressing that whatever was done must be done with such thoughts in mind, were shocked when they read Chesterfield's *Letters to His Son.* Chesterfield's letters were written with the sole purpose of instructing his sons in the ways of the world, and while several letters were concerned with religion and morality, he nevertheless felt that these things should be left to their tutors.

Samuel Johnson said that the letters taught "the morals of a whore and the manners of a dancingmaster," a statement that was repeated many times in preference to his more favorable comment that if the immorality were taken out "the book should be in the hands of every gentleman." It was in the nature of Johnson's latter comment that America accepted the *Letters.* They were published many times and in many forms, often under the title of *Principles of Polite-*

ness. Passages were reprinted in school readers, newspapers, and etiquette books of the day, and it was soon to become the most popular manual on manners.

"Next to good-breeding," said Chesterfield, "is genteel manners and carriage," and the best method to acquire these is through a knowledge of dance.

> Now to acquire a graceful air, you must attend to your dancing; no one can either sit, stand or walk well, unless he dances well. And in learning to dance, be particularly attentive to the motion of your arms for a stiffness in the wrist will make any man look awkward. If a man walks well, presents himself well in company, wears his hat well, moves his head properly, and his arms gracefully, it is almost all that is necessary.[70]

It was the task of the dancing masters to see that these qualities that were valued so much by Chesterfield were taught to their students. It is difficult to state the precise method used by certain dancing masters although they often stated in their advertisements that they taught "according to the newest French manner" or "after the newest and politest manner practised in London, Dublin, and Paris."

It is known by examinations of old inventories that some of the books on the art of dancing had come from England and were to be found in the libraries of both dancing master and layman. The inventory of Charles Stagg, a Williamsburg dancing master, shows "a Book the art of Dancing by J. Weaver, and Do by J. Essex."[71] Both Weaver and John Essex were well known dancing masters in London, and both translated Raoul Ager Feuillet's *Choregraphie, ou l'Art d'écrire la Danse,* which they called *The Art of Dancing.* The book was concerned with a system of dance notation which Feuillet had invented. Nicholas Scanlan advertised in the *South Carolina Gazette* in 1751 that someone had borrowed or taken "a book of high dances," which had been written especially for him by "Mynheer *Brockhurst* of the academy at *Amsterdam*" and therefore would be of no use to anyone else.[72]

In the library of Robert Beverly could be found "Ye 2nd Vol. of ye Dancing Master." [73] This no doubt was a translation of Rameau's *Maître à Danser,* which today is considered the standard work concerning the technique of eighteenth-century dancing. *The Dancing Master* was written by Pierre Rameau, and first published in Paris in 1725. In 1728, John Essex issued in London the first English translation of the book.[74] By an examination of the book some knowledge may be gained as to what was considered essential in learning the art of dancing. The book deals mainly with ballroom dancing, although some mention is made of theatrical dancing.

Rameau states that he has prepared the book in such a manner that the "master may train his pupil in one step after another, at the same time teaching him the different movements of the arms which are appropriate to the various steps in dancing." The first step the pupil must learn is the correct manner of holding the body. For if the body is well placed, it is then "ready to perform whatever may be required . . . whether you wish to walk, bow or dance." This position was considered most important and was one of the main reasons for the study of dance. As for the position he states:

> The head must be held erect without any suggestion of stiffness, the shoulders pressed well back, for this expands the chest and affords more grace to the body. The arms should hang at the side, the hands be neither quite open nor quite closed, the waist steady, the legs straight and the feet turned outwards.[75]

In taking this position, one should avoid appearing stiff or awkward as this is as bad as affectation.

The next important step that should be learned is the proper manner of walking, for on this "depends the first requisite for dancing." The method which Rameau describes for walking is easy because only natural movements are used. After one has learned to walk well, he then should learn the five positions (these are the same as those of ballet, only less in degree) and as these differ only in the position of the legs and feet, the body should at all times be held "upright and supported on both feet." [76]

The next chapter deals with "Honors in General" and the proper method of taking off and putting on one's hat and making a graceful bow. While less care and attention is given to them, Rameau insists that they both should be done well. After taking up the "Manner of Behaving Genteely at Formal Balls," he discusses the various steps used in dance and describes the steps and manner of dancing the minuet, courante, gailliard, rigadoon, and gavotte. [77]

In reading the description of the various steps, one soon realizes that they are the same steps used in ballet and stage dancing today, differing only in degree. For Rameau describes how to do a *demi-coupe* or half-cut, *jetés* or jumps, pirouettes and many others. It was these steps that were used in the minuet and other dances of the day. No wonder a dancing master was engaged if one desired to learn to dance. It would have been difficult to learn any other way.

The second part of the book is "A Discourse on the Arms and of the Importance of Knowing how to Move Them Gracefully." Of the arms Rameau states that "nothing is more advantageous to those who have an aptitude for dancing and a disposition to dance well, than to apply themselves to the study of the proper carriage of the arms." [78] This is most important, because no matter how well a person may perform the steps, if he desires his dance to appear full of life he must have soft and graceful arms. Each step in the dance has a certain corresponding movement of the shoulder, arm, wrist, and hand, which if not done correctly would have the same effect on the beholder as "a picture without a frame."

As one studies Rameau's *The Dancing Master,* it becomes evident what strict discipline was taught and was considered so necessary for the young lady and gentleman. Although dancing often fell under the heading of recreation or accomplishment, its main purpose was to teach its pupils deportment and how to move gracefully, so that they might prove to everyone that they were young ladies and gentlemen. That dancing was not learned entirely for the pleasure that was received by the dancer is indicated by an incident that characterized the Philadelphia Assembly in 1781.

> "Come, miss, have a care what you are doing," shouted the Master of Ceremonies to a damsel who was permitting a bit of gossip to interrupt her turn in a contradance. "Do you think you are here for your own pleasure?" [79]

This strictness in discipline is shown also in Fithian's account of Mr. Christian's dancing class:

> The Dance continued til two, we dined at half after three— soon after Dinner we repaired to the Dancing-Room again; I observed in the course of the lesson, that Mr. Christian is punctual, and rigid in his discipline, so strict indeed that he struck two of the young Misses for a fault in the course of their performance, even in the presence of the Mother of one of them! And he rebuked one of the Young Fellows as highly as to tell him he must alter his manner, which he had

observed in the Course of the Dance, to be insolent, and wanton, or absent himself from the school. . . .[80]

There was no better way for the young to learn genteel manners and a graceful carriage than by studying a year or so with the dancing master. Jedediah Huntington wrote to his brother in 1783 that he was pleased to hear that they had a dancing school; for if the dancing master was a "well-bred man, he would be of eminent Service to the Manners & Sentiments of his Pupils. . . ."[81] In Philadelphia, Theobald Hackett, a dancing master who had recently come from England and Ireland, advertised that he had opened a dancing school and that he not only taught all the fashionable dances of England and France but would "give all young ladies, gentlemen, and children (that please to learn of him) the most graceful carriage in dancing, and genteel behavior in company, that can possibly be given by any dancing master whatever."[82] A merchant from Boston, in hopes of giving his daughter the best education, sent her to school in the city "to be taught needlework and dancing, and to improve her manners in good and genteel company."[83]

Learning to dance and the other elegant accomplishments was felt to put a young girl in such a shining light that it was no trouble at all for her to attract a husband. In a "Dialogue between a Preceptor of an Academy and Parent of an Offered Pupil" this fact is brought out. The preceptor believed in first pursuing the solid branches while the parent felt that he had given his fourteen-year-old daughter the best education by sending her to the capital, to enjoy all the advantages it had to offer. The parent says:

I boarded her a year in the capital, where she enjoyed every possible advantage. She attended the most accomplished masters in the ornamental branches of science; visited the

genteelest families, and frequented all the scenes of amusements. It is true, her letters are not always quite so accur-
ately as could be wished; yet she dances well, plays well
on piano-forte, and sings like a nightingale.

The preceptor then asked if she knew the domestic accomplishments, and is capable of cooking and patching for her
husband "should she ever be so lucky to get one." To this
the parent replies, "Her accomplishments will command her
a husband as soon as she wishes." [84]

Some of the parents thought not only that dancing was
necessary for girls but boys also should learn dancing before
learning a trade. Two schoolboys give their parents ideas on
dancing as they discuss the subject.

> *Harry:* Tom, when are you going to begin your dancing?
> You will be so old in a short time as to be ashamed to be
> seen taking your five positions.
> *Thomas:* I don't know as I shall begin at all. Father says he
> don't care a fig whether I learn to jump any better than I
> do now; and, as I am to be a tradesman, he is determined,
> at present, to keep me at the reading and writing
> schools.
> *Harry:* That must be very dull and dry for you. And what
> good will all such learning do you, so long as you make
> the awkward appearance you do at present? I am sur-
> prised at your father's folly. So, because you are to be a
> *tradesman,* you are not to learn the graces! I expect to
> learn a trade too. But papa says I shall first learn the
> *dancing trade;* and then, if I never learn any other, I shall
> make my way through the world well enough.[85]

Noah Webster agreed with the preceptor and Thomas'
father. He believed that the fatal mistake in the education
of females, which was "illustrated in every large town in
America," was the following of England and France in their

elegant manners and amusements. Such an education as music, dancing, and drawing would be fatal to domestic happiness, because it made a "disproportion between well-bred females and the males in our large towns." When the boys were sent to their fathers' shops or were apprenticed to a mechanic, the girls were sent to a boarding school "where their ideas are elevated and their views carried above the connections with men in those occupations." [86]

Webster believed, as did many others who wrote on the proper education for a republic, that it should be nationalistic. It was his belief that the greatest evil in America was that the refinement of manners had reached a point its wealth could not support. America, being a new country, had reached that stage of development where its education should be such that "every youth must be instructed in the business by which he is to procure subsistence." [87] France and England, being older, had progressed "from simplicity to corruption" where "even the civilities of behavior in polished society, becomes a science; a bow and a curtsey were taught with as much care and precision as the elements of Mathematics." Therefore, thought Webster, girls should be given more of the basic curriculum; and dance, music, and drawing should hold a subordinate rank. After all, "no man marries a woman for her performance on a harpiscord, or her figure in a minuet"; he marries a woman who can preside over a home and the education of their children. [88]

Webster, however, was not against dancing, for he often frequented balls and assemblies and while in New York, as editor of the *American Magazine*, he had taken "a few steps in dancing under Mr. Hulet." [89]

Benjamin Rush, another advocate for nationalistic education, believed that dancing should be a part of the education of the American lady because it promoted health and made

the movements of the body easy and graceful. In his
*Sermons to the Rich and Studious on Temperance and
Exercise,* he wrote:

> Dancing is a salutary exercise. Future ages will be surprised
> to hear that rational creatures should, at any time, have
> looked upon it as a criminal amusement. To reason against
> it, from its abuse, concludes equally strong against the law-
> fulness of every thing we hold sacred and valuable in life.
> . . . By its mechanical effects on the body, it inspires the
> mind with cheerfulness, and this, when well founded, and
> properly restrained, is another name for religion. . . . The
> music, which always accompanies this exercise, hath a pleas-
> ing and salutary effect upon the body as well as the mind.
> . . . Dancing should not be used more than once or twice a
> week. It should never be continued 'till weariness comes on,
> nor should we expose ourselves to the cold air too soon
> after it.[90]

Much of Rush's statement on dancing was later to be found
in the *Minor Encyclopedia, or Cabinet of General Knowledge,* printed in Boston in 1803, and still later in Durang's
Ball-Room Bijou, and Art of Dancing, published in Philadelphia about 1855.

Education in America had its beginning in the schools
founded by religious organizations. They set the laws of the
school as well as the curriculum. Their aim, first and fore-
most, was to provide enough reading and writing that the
young might understand the Bible and sermons, and then
stand in the fear of God. The colleges were set up to provide
education for an enlightened ministry. As the eighteenth
century progressed and men changed their attitudes towards
religion, this change was reflected in the education of its
nation's youth. Private schools were set up that held no
religious connections. Public education was for paupers or

orphans, the upper and middle classes sent their children to private or church schools for which they paid tuition. If a parent felt that dance should play a part in the education of his child, he sent him to schools that included dance in their program, or the child was instructed in the art in a private dancing school or by a tutor.

Higher education throughout the century still remained in the hands of or under the influence of religious organizations. The greater number of colleges could not see dance as a part of the program, and some forbade the students to go outside the college to receive instruction. However, toward the end of the century, commencement balls had found their way into college life, and despite restriction against dancing, some students ventured to a dancing school or private or public ball.

As early as 1722 there was a complaint of what the students at Harvard were learning. Benjamin Franklin, writing under the name of Silence Dogood, complained that the students "learned little more than how to carry themselves handsomely, and enter a Room genteely, (which might as well be acquir'd at a Dancing School). . . ."[91]

Under the administration of President Wadsworth (1725–37) the Overseers of Harvard recommended to the Corporation "to pass an act to restrain unsuitable and unreasonable dancings in the College."[92] While the Reverend Edward Holyoke (1737–69) was president, the Corporation voted in 1760, "That there shall be no Dancing allow'd on any part of Com[m]encent Week, either in the College-Hall or Chapel." Although this rule was written in the College Book, it seems to have done little good, for the same restriction was written again seven years later, with punishments added for those who broke the rule. Possibly because of the rule, two graduates of the class of 1767, issued an invitation "to a Dance at the Town House on Thursday after Commencement." [93]

According to John Adams' diary, the commencement at Harvard still included dancing in 1771, for Sister Cranch, having gone to the commencement and made many observations, had now "altered her mind about dancing and dancing-schools," while Mr. Cranch was convinced "that all such as learn to dance are so taken up with it, that they can't be students." [94]

The authorities at Princeton also showed their disapproval of dancing. When they learned that a French dancing master had set up a school at one of the local taverns which was being frequented by the students, they unanimously resolved that the students should be forbidden to attend. Their reason was that it hurt the reputation of the college and was "unfriendly to order and good government." [95] Some of the undergraduates agreed with the authorities in their disapproval of this dancing school. Zadock Squire, one of the undergraduates, wrote to a friend that—

> We have a dancing master in town, and a fencing master, and I do not know what other animal, but I believe it would be better for us if these frenchmen were all where they came from; for a republick cannot subsist by such useless accomplishments; it must subsist only by simplicity and frugality. [96]

In spite of this attitude, the students desired to dance, and sometime later won the right to have an annual ball. Many of the graduates would have been shocked had they seen the undergraduates of 1786, "dancing up and down the entry as a Negro played upon a violin with 'twenty students hallooing and tearing about.'" [97]

Fithian wrote to John Peck, a Princeton student who was about to succeed him as tutor at Nomine Hall, advising him that "any young Gentleman travelling through the Colony, as I have said before, is presumed to be acquainted with dancing. . . ." Fithian also advised Peck that from the beginning he should convince his scholars of his ability, but that would not be hard to do as he had gone through the usual course at Princeton where he had learned the basic languages, mathematics, and the other required course, and beside had "learned a smattering of Dancing, card, &c. &c. &c." [98]

While at Yale, Ebenezer Baldwin wrote in his diary that ". . . Nicholas, Halliock, and Brewester were publickly admonished for having a Dance at Milford, and for their general conduct." Three others were also fined for being at the same dance.[99] Twenty years later, President Ezra Stiles, gave his consent that some of the scholars could attend the dancing school in town. They were allowed to go in the evenings and on Thursday afternoon "but not to interrupt any College Exercises." He also sent his own children to the dancing school, but the school was short-lived because there was "Great Dissatisfaction about the School of polite manners called the dancing School." [100]

At Dartmouth, in 1771, the members of the sophomore and freshman class sent a petition to the authorities asking if they might not spend some of their hours of leisure in "stepping the minuet, and learning the sword." [101] Four years later at the University of Pennsylvania, Benjamin Franklin's grandson wrote to his father:

> I will now leave you to judge whether there is any time left for either Dancing or Fencing. I think there is none except Saturday afternoon in which to be sure I might go to Dancing School. That would be but once in the Week and perhaps it would be enough to retain what I know of it. But this I will leave entirely to you and if it meets with your appro-

bation I will desire Dr. Ellision to free me from my Saturday's tasks as I think I shall not be able to dance with so much spirit when the thoughts of making a Latin theme is sticking in my stomach.[102]

Franklin, in reply to his son's letter, said he had no fault to find with dancing.

Where northern colleges tended to pass laws against dancing and forbid their students to frequent dancing school, the southern colleges encouraged it. It is not surprising to find that dance was supported and encouraged by the College of William and Mary, since dance played such a part in the life and education of the south. It must be remembered that William and Mary tried to follow the same course as did the colleges in England. Although many of the planters still sent their sons to England to be educated, it was with the desire that they would acquire the polish and culture the English aristocracy had to offer. Only when the southern colleges could offer those things which were thought necessary in the education of a gentleman would they ever hope to compete with the larger universities of England.

According to the English idea, a student must not only have a knowledge of the basic courses but must also know how to dance gracefully. One of the subjects that Hugh Jones, a teacher at William and Mary, suggests should be taught at the college were the accomplishments, which included music, dancing, and fencing. These should be taught by the "town masters" at such times as the president and masters appointed. [103] In 1716, the college granted William Livingston permission to use a room in the college "for teaching the Scholars and others to dance until his own dancing school in Williamsburg be finished." [104] Later, in 1737, William Dering advertised that he had "opened his school at the college, where all Gentlemen's Sons may be taught Dancing, according to the newest *French* Manner." [105]

By the end of the century balls and dancing schools were attended by college students, both north and south, and the contribution of dance toward a man's becoming a better member of society was attested by many who were later to become well known.

III

As people learned the dances and manners of "High Society," they called for more balls and assemblies where they might put their new skills to use. But just as the dancing schools caused a rise in the number of balls and assemblies, so the number of balls and assemblies caused a rise in the number of dancing schools. Each was dependent on the other.

The balls and assemblies played an important part in the social world. A correspondent to the *Pittsburgh Gazette* complained to its editor:

> To what a height this contagious distemper is arrived . . . is but too visible. Every village which has the least pretension to gentility, has its assembly. . . . Singing, dancing, fiddling, and gaming, are no longer mere amusements, they are ranked among the important occupations of the day, among the principle duties of human beings.[106]

In spite of such complaints and others that protested against the great number of assemblies, they continued. Many of them had a definite purpose, like the assembly given at Boston in 1769, by Henry Hulton, Commissioner of Customs. His sister, Ann, wrote of the occasion in a letter to a friend stating that the Commissioner had started an assembly "in order to wear off the prejudice of the people & to cultivate their Acquaintance." [107]

Before the Revolution, there were balls to celebrate the king's birthday. The people of Philadelphia could read an account in the *Pennsylvania Mercury* of such a ball that was given in New York. It was a gala occasion, as the day was celebrated by drinking healths to His Majesty and the royal family, the building of bonfires and the shooting of fireworks, and the day was concluded with a ball given by His Excellency the Governor.[108] After the Revolution, it was the custom to celebrate George Washington's birthday in much the same manner.

Although the Declaration of Independence declared "that all men are created equal," there was still a class consciousness, and at the balls this could readily be seen. Before 1775, one of the highest honors was to receive an invitation to the Royal Governor's ball, and usually only those who had some rank were invited. After the War of Independence when titles were no longer in fashion, invitations to the balls were based on professional standing. "There is great snobbery in Philadelphia, where the classes are sharply divided," wrote Moreau de Saint-Mery in his *American Journey*. He continues by saying: "This is particularly noticeable at balls. There are some balls where no one is admitted unless his professional standing is up to a certain mark." One ball ended in fisticuffs, as insults passed between a small jeweler and a hairdresser.[109]

Noah Webster found the same situation with Philadelphia society. When he attended the assembly, he found that the ladies would not dance with strangers and such action caused him to comment that "People in high life suppose they have a right to dispense with rules of civility." In the same month he had been at Wilmington and was disappointed with the ball because he did not know the rules. However, a month earlier he had been in Annapolis and had found the "assembly brilliant" with "a brilliant circle of ladies." [110]

In 1799, Washington declined the invitation to the assemblies at Alexandria because his age and health would not permit him to dance; however he wished the best for those that did attend.[111] A month later, the managers of the Hartford Assembly requested that in deference to Washington's death the "ladies dress in white trimmed in black, and the Gentlemen wear a crape on the arm for the evening." [112]

In the South, those who lived on the plantations would usually give their own lavish balls, which lasted for days. Fithian states many times in his *Journal* that the Carter family, or certain members of it, had gone to Stratford or Mr. Tuberville's to a ball. In describing a ball at which he had accompanied Mrs. Carter, he said:

> About Seven the Ladies & Gentlemen began to dance in the Ball-Room. first Minuets one Round; Second Giggs; third Reels; and last of all Country-Dances; tho' they struck several Marches occasionally—The Music was a French Horn and two Violins.[113]

Many of the assemblies were conducted by dancing teachers. It was by this method that they gained new students and also supplemented their income. William Dering, a dancing teacher in Williamsburg, informed the gentlemen and ladies at the capitol that he would hold an assembly every other night during court.[114] Where there was more than one dancing teacher in town, there often was rivalry to see who could give the most handsome ball.

In Williamsburg, Mrs. Stagg advertised in March, 1738, that she would give an Assembly at the capital on the 27th of April at which "several grotesque dances never yet performed in Virginia" would be given and also "several valuable Goods will be put up to be Raffled for; also a likely young negro Fellow." In the next issue of the *Gazette* Mrs. De Graffeneidt advertised that she would give a ball the 26th of April and an assembly the 28th. There is no doubt that Mrs. De Graffeneidt saw Mrs. Staggs' announcement of a raffle of a "young negro fellow" and not to be outdone she added the following note to her advertisement: "There will be set up to be Raffled for, a likely young *Virginia* Negro Woman, fit for House Business, and her Child." Mr. Parks, the editor of the *Gazette,* apparently realized the rivalry between the two dance teachers, for he diplomatically changed the position of the advertisements with each issue, putting first one on top and then the other.[115]

The dancing masters often gave balls for their scholars. Mr. Pike, who taught in Charleston, South Carolina, gave an annual ball for his scholars, while Dering and Scanlan, of the same city, gave a ball for their scholars' parents.[116] At these balls the pupils often showed the latest dances. In New Haven, Mr. Lançon gave a public ball at which his pupils performed "the newest and most fashionable Dances." [117]

While the people of society were concerned over their invitations to the assemblies, the plainer folk, who could not even hope for such invitations, danced for the fun of dancing. They learned the dances from an older member of the group rather than from a dancing school. Saint-Mery says:

> I have already said elsewhere that dancing for the inhabitants of the United States is less a matter of self-display than it is true enjoyment. At the same dance you will see a

grandfather, his son and his grandson, but more often still the grandmother, her daughter and grand-daughter. If a Frenchman comments upon this with surprise he is told that one dances for his own amusement, and not because it is the thing to do.[118]

One of the favorite ways of getting together was the bee, or frolic, of which there were many kinds. The bee or frolic had a purpose and combined work with pleasure. Several farmers and their wives and children would go to one farm to help a neighbor with his work, and after the work was done they would all have a hearty meal and dance. "The name 'Frolic,'" says St. John De Crevecoeur,

> may perhaps scandalize you and make you imagine that we meet to riot together. Lest you should misunderstand me, give me leave to explain myself. I really know among us of no custom which is so useful and tends so much to establish the union and the little society which subsists among us. Poor as we are, if we have not the gorgeous balls, the harmonious concerts, the shrill horn of Europe, yet we dilate our hearts as well with the simple negro fiddle. . . .[119]

In Virginia, as elsewhere, fairs were established to encourage trade and promote general commerce. As a means to encourage the people to attend and bring their wares and livestock, entertainment and diversions were provided as well as prizes. At the Williamsburg Fair among the prizes contended for were "a pair of Pumps to be danc'd for by men." [120]

Peter Cartwright, whose "delight was in dancing" before be became a minister, tells of his early life in Logan County, Kentucky, where Sunday was considered the day of recreation and at such times balls and dances were given and attended with jollity and mirth. Marriages were also an occasion for dancing.[121]

While the Negroes were often called upon to play and call the dances at the balls, they were not without their own dances, oftentimes copied from the white people. Sundays, after they had been to church in their finest clothes, they often spent in dancing. According to Saint- Mery the Negroes had a "mania" for dancing.[122]

While there were few dancing schools and balls at the beginning of the eighteenth century, the century closed with dancing schools and balls playing an important part in American society. As the dancing teacher moved from city to hamlet and taught either in his own school or in a boarding school or academy, he gradually made a place for himself, as he proved the value of dance as a means of educating the youth in bodily exercises, and a means of acquiring grace and manners, as well as an elegant recreation, all of which was thought to be necessary by the best educational writers of the day.

PART THREE

Dance Education in the Nineteenth Century

AMERICA during the nineteenth century was a nation of vast growth and development and many changes took place. At the beginning of the century, the majority of the people still lived their provincial lives close to the Atlantic coast. The census of 1800 gave the population at 5,308,483, with the center of population 18 miles west of Baltimore. The Mississippi River marked the western boundary at the beginning of the century, but Jefferson doubled the land area when he signed the Louisiana Purchase Treaty in 1803 and bought the Louisiana Territory from France. In the same year he had given instructions to Meriwether Lewis and William Clark to form an exploring expedition to investigate the resources of the Territory. In 1805 the Lewis and Clark expedition went beyond the Louisiana Territory, into the Oregon Country and finally to the Pacific. Throughout the century more land was acquired and by 1900, 46 of the 48 states had been admitted to the Union. The population had grown because of both a great number of immigrants and a high birth rate.

Despite the vast acres of land that had been added by Jefferson during his administration, travel was poor. The few roads became muddy in the spring and fall and dusty in the summer. Travel, during the early years of the century was usually by horseback or horse-drawn vehicles, while those who were going between the coastal towns went by water. To help speed the slow process of goods from the back country, men began to experiment with steam. In 1807,

Robert Fulton's steamboat, the *Clermont,* began its first trip up the Hudson from New York to Albany. Ten years later steam navigation on the Mississippi River had definitely begun when the steamboat *Washington* made round trips from Louisville to New Orleans.

The building of canals did much to facilitate transportation during the following years. To aid overland travel a system of turnpikes was started. In 1831, the first steam-drawn locomotive went between Albany and Schenectady and thus began what was to become later a major factor in opening up of new lands and territories. During the last decade of the century, with the invention of the automobile, transportation had vastly changed from the poor roads and horse-drawn vehicles of a hundred years earlier.

America in 1800 was an agricultural nation with a few large cities. Due to the many inventions and discoveries which not only helped the manufacturer and the farmer but also the housewife, America was slowly becoming an industrial nation. With greater industrial development, came "Big Business" and the "American City," and by 1900 America had changed from an agrarian nation to an industrial nation.

As America began to produce its own writers, artists, and musicians, it began to sever its cultural dependence on Europe. The arts began to show a distinctive form of expression that spoke both for and of America. The growing interest in music and the theatre was seen as the larger cities began to form their own symphony orchestras and theatres. America was also producing its own ballet dancers, although it still leaned heavily on Europe, and it was not until the next century that a truly American ballet was formed.

Religious ideas were also changing. While religion was still a most important factor in man's life, it did not dominate him. However, the century was not without its revivals.

Starting with the Second Awakening in the East, it spread to the West where it took on a more colorful nature with its camp meetings that lasted for days. Throughout the first half of the century, there were many local revivals which finally culminated in the "Great Revival of 1858."

Among the worldly sins that often brought on discussion at these revivals was dancing. Cartwright, the great Methodist itinerant preacher of the west, delights in telling of the many dances he successfully interrupted. He also tells how the Methodist of the west at the beginning of the century wore plain and simple clothes and attended church regularly and "did not allow their children to go to balls or plays; they did not send them to dancing-schools"; and those who persisted in attending dancing schools or dances were often publicly admonished or excommunicated.[1]

After the panic of 1857 came the "Great Awakening" which turned peoples' minds toward religion. In New York, as in other cities, there was "prayer meeting morning, noon and night . . . prayer meeting in town, village and hamlet, North and South." Dancing was considered among the deadly sins "according to the ethics of this revival"[2] Even the youth felt the wave of revival for in 1860 three little girls, who had recently united with the church, felt that they should begin "practical Christian work." This work took the form of distributing tracts among the neglected classes, and one of the tracts distributed was titled *The Social Evils of Dancing, Card Playing and Theatre-going.*[3]

At the Princeton Theological Seminary, the students were taught that manners were important to the clergyman, but not the manners that were practiced by those who followed the Chesterfieldian code, which among other things artificial and worldly, "qualified their possessors to make a distinguished figure in a ballroom, or at the levee of a great man." They were warned not to allow themselves to be present at places where cards or dancing were a part of the entertainment and if such a thing should happen, even at the most intimate family parties, they were to excuse themselves.[4]

While the greatest number of ministers felt that dancing was worldly and could lead only to hell, some, like the Shakers, felt that it should form a part of the religious service. In Ohio, in the early part of the century, the Schismatics departed from the New Lights, because they believed in voluntary exercise of dancing. Galbraith states:

> . . . the principal thing that distinguished the Schismatic worship from that of the New Lights, was their taking privilege of exhibiting, by bold faith, what others were moved to by a blind impulse. This, they considered a great advancement in the spirit of the revival; and upon this principle, the voluntary exercise of dancing was introduced as the worship of God . . .

and so the Schismatics encouraged "one another to praise God in the dance."[5]

Dr. W. E. Channing, Unitarian minister at Boston, was in agreement with other ministers that balls were one of the worst forms of social pleasure with their late hours, their extravagance of dress, and exposure of health. In an address before the Massachusetts Temperance Society, he desired that dance should become such a part of everyday life that no special preparation was necessary; that families should use it as a means of "exercise and exhilaration." He also believed that if it were extended to the laboring classes it would prove not only an innocent pleasure but a way for the improvement of manners. Therefore, if such an innocent pleasure were afforded the laboring classes, it would be a means of temperance among those who are most exposed to intemperance.[6]

In the last decade of the nineteenth century, dancing was still denounced, although it had gained more advocates both among the ministry and laity. In 1894 *The New York Times* took a survey of the attitudes of the ministers towards dancing and stated that:

> Among the clergymen the division is as marked and as profound as it is among the laity. There are clergymen of the liberal school who not merely attend balls given by their parishioners but who applaud the waltz and the polka, and deny the responsibility of harm being inherent in either of them.
>
> On the other hand, many clergymen, both of New York and Brooklyn, make no effort to conceal their opposition to all forms and varieties of public dancing, and especially the dances [waltz and polka] so vehemently denounced at the Brooklyn revival.[7]

One of the ministers of the liberal school was Dr. Stoddard, rector of St. John's Protestant Episcopal Church in Jersey City, New Jersey, who considered opening a dancing school under the direction of the church officials. He had permitted dancing in the church gymnasium before, and thought that if young people were going to dance, it would be better to throw a safeguard around them. He saw dancing as wholesome exercise and a means of promoting graceful movement and carriage of the body.[8]

The main reason given against dancing by the ministers and the host of anti-dance books that issued from the presses was directed to the upper classes: that great expense in both time and money was spent on the preparation for a ball, either public or private. The preparation included expensive dress and jewelry, the service, and even the furniture; and this expense grew greater as each tried to outdo the other in giving the most lavish ball. Another reason given was the harmful effects upon health of those who danced: the late hours; entering the cool night air before becoming sufficiently cooled; the using up of the oxygen in the room and thereby breathing foul air; and also the mental and physical excitement caused by a ball. Its evil influences upon intellectual improvement and its moral and religious aspects were other reasons given against dance as practiced among the upper classes. Among the lower classes, dance was associated in the minds of the ministers and reformers with the cheap dance halls that sold liquor and had gambling rooms and prostitutes.

Although the clergymen and reformers censured dance, the greater number agreed that if it were used outdoors as an exercise, where there was nothing to excite the emotions, rather than for its conventional purpose, it would be a healthful pastime. But they all were quick to state that they were not "discussing dance as it might be, but dance as it is." [9]

Despite the many attacks on dance, it was not without its champions. Newspapers and magazines published pictures and descriptions of the latest evening wear for the ballroom. Many reported on the fashionable dances of Paris, London, New York, Philadelphia, the presidential balls, and the cadet hops at West Point. Books describing how to do the latest dances in the most acceptable manner came from the presses as fast as the anti-dance books. Etiquette books contained chapters on the correct manner of entering a ballroom and the proper deportment for those who attended. They also gave the proper manner of conducting a ball. Because dance refined the manners and often was used as an entrance into fashionable society "self-help" books saw it as a valuable and elegant accomplishment.

"Probably more 'light fantastic toes' will be sported this season than ever trod the ball-room floor before . . ." wrote the editor of *Ballou's Pictorial Drawing-Room Companion.* He went on to say that where religious prejudices had once forbidden dance and classed it with drinking and dicing, such prejudices are fast passing away.[10] The editor of *Harper's New Monthly Magazine* wrote, "The gravity of the discussion of the morality of dancing is exceedingly amusing." Because he saw dancing of the young people as natural and instinctive, he "might as wisely quarrel with the song of the bobolink in the field as with the dance upon the floor." [11]

The Young Lady's Book, printed in 1830 and copied after the English publication of the same name, had a chapter on dancing, telling its history and giving written and graphic description of exercises that "will tend to improve those who are deficient and to confirm those who are correct." [12] This same chapter was published in *Godey's Lady's Book* for August and October, 1831. *Godey's Lady's Book* did much towards popularizing and breaking down prejudice against dance by publishing descriptions and pictures of the latest ballgowns, the dances and music. Mrs. Sarah Jane Hale, the editor of the magazine, showed her approval of dancing by offering it as a subject in her own boarding school in Philadelphia.

"The morality of round dances seems now to be little questioned," wrote Mrs. Sherwood in the fourth edition of *Manners and Social Usages.* "At any rate, young girls in the presence of their mothers are not supposed to come to harm from their enjoyment." [13] It was the introduction of the round dances, starting first with the waltz and then the polka, that had provided new fuel for the fire that blazed against dance. Not only ministers and moralists protested against such licentious dances, but newspapers, magazines, and old-timers wrote to tell of their evils. Even dancing masters censured the dances when improperly taught.

The waltz was introduced into America towards the beginning of the century and so shocked some of the people that they forbade their sons and daughters to dance it. Senator John Tyler, who later became president, first saw the waltz in 1827, and wrote his daughter that he found it a "dance which you have never seen, and which I do not desire to see you dance. It is rather vulgar I think." [14] Mme. Celnart wrote in *The Gentleman and Lady's Book of Politeness:*

> The waltz is a dance of quite too loose a character, and unmarried ladies should refrain from it in public and private; very young married ladies, however, may be allowed to waltz in private balls, if it is very seldom and with persons of their acquaintance. It is indispensable for them to acquit themeslves with dignity and decency. [15]

This book was translated from the French and became very popular, going through fifteen editions between 1833 and 1872.

The *Boston Weekly Magazine* stated in poetry its dislike of the waltz.

> . . . They rise, they twirl, they swing, they fly,
> Puffing, blowing, jostling, squeezing,
> Very odd, but very pleasing—
> 'Till every Lady plainly shows
> (Whatever else she may disclose)
> Reserve is not among her faults:—
> Reader this is to waltz. [16]

Despite the attacks, the waltz continued in popularity and by 1885 Dodworth could write that "We have now arrived at the culmination of modern society dancing, the dance which has for fifty years resisted every kind of attack, and is today the most popular known."[17] However, if one chose to waltz then certain rules of decorum must be followed. The gentlemen were informed that they were not to encircle the waist of the lady until the dance had begun. It was taboo for a gentleman to put his bare hand on the waist of a lady, if he happened to be without his gloves then he could use a handkerchief in his hand.

The polka excited even more attention than did the waltz. It was first danced in America by L. DeGarmo Brooks and Mary Ann Gannon at the National Theatre in New York, on May 10, 1844, and was introduced into fashionable society the same year by Gabriel De Korponay and Mademoiselle Pauline Desjardins. It was a dance that the Prince Consort had forbidden to be danced in the presence of Queen Victoria. George Templeton Strong on seeing the polka for the first time said, "It's a kind of insane Tartar jig performed to a disagreeable music of an uncivilized character." Two years later he was so disgusted with the polka that he wrote in his diary, "Wish I had the man here that invented the polka—I'd scrape him to death with oyster shells."[18]

While visiting a friend in New York, Mary Cosby Shelby, granddaughter of Kentucky's Governor Shelby, was invited to watch her friend as she took a polka lesson. Mary wrote of the occasion in her journal:

At nine Georgia Edwards came around, said she intended taking a Polka lesson, & would be glad for Sue & I to go with her. It seems to be greatly in vogue here. I never before saw it danced. It is a graceful pretty dance, and Georgia danced it very gracefully. But I have the same objections to seeing a Lady and gentleman dance it that I have to the waltz. And nothing would induce me to learn it.[19]

The round dances somehow characterized the age of the common man. They were less formal than the minuet; they were wild, reckless, daring and, above all, fast, as was this new age of faster transportation and modern machinery. As the younger generation whirled in the waltz, polka, and galop, the older folk wondered what the world was coming to. When the young gentlemen put their arms about the ladies' waists and whirled them about the room, the older generation warned the girls that they would lose all modesty and self-respect, and predicted where such intimacies would lead.

The round dances were not difficult to learn and thereby brought about a change in the teaching of dance. The steps themselves, being simple, could be learned by watching them danced. Only a few lessons with a dance teacher were necessary to learn the steps. This fact worried many of the older dancing masters whose prime objective was to teach the student the graceful use of the body and the deportment of the ballroom. They complained of the teachers who only taught steps and dances without teaching those other "little things" that were so important to the dancing master of the previous generation.

Allen Dodworth, who opened his dancing academy about 1835 in New York and taught there over fifty years, watched with regret the many changes that were taking place in the teaching of dance. His book *Dancing and Its Relation to Education and Social Life* is a classic in the field of social dancing. He gives some idea of the effect that the round dances had on dance and dance education, when he states:

With the introduction of the waltz, galop and other round dances, a complete revolution in social dancing took place. These were so easily learned that the education in motion was deemed unnecessary; simply to make the motion required was quite sufficient, manner becoming entirely secondary. Many learned from one to the other, frequently transmitting their own mistakes. . . . [The new dance teachers] not having had the advantages of the teachings and associations of the older ones, they were not aware of the proper nature of their duties; but they were able to waltz expertly, and the teaching of the waltz and a few other dances was all they believed to be required of them; they were, therefore, simply dance teachers, not teachers of motion and manner, which is the definition of dancing-master as the term was formerly understood.[20]

Such teaching brought with it a loss of the modesty and manner that should accompany those who dance. This loss accompanied them to the drawing rooms and ballrooms and was transmitted to those with whom they danced and its consequence was "a deterioration in the general tone of motion and manner."

II

Early in the century, the American people began to realize that they were no longer tied to Britain but were free to develop their wealth of natural resources as they wished. Business became their prime objective. Whatever one did must aid in his business, whether it was education, religion, recreation or even dancing. Therefore, the dancing master presented dance as a means of gaining greater wealth and prestige.

In 1810, a Boston dancing master wrote that not only was it the task of the "modern" dancing master to "teach the feet how to tread," but also it was his duty to fix and establish in youth those thousand little items of character and behavior which are so far from being trifles that they decide and stamp the man; they procure for him future reception and favor among mankind, and too often determine through life his prosperity and safety, that more men have made their fortunes by a graceful and manly appearance, than by their knowledge of the arts and sciences.[21]

"By all means, take lessons in dancing," advised T. S. Arthur, in *Advice to Young Men.* He believed that such an accomplishment was necessary if one wanted to "give or receive all the benefits that spring from right intercourse." [22]

To say that everybody felt like the Boston dancing master or T. S. Arthur would be false. Many felt as did another writer who entitled his book *Advice to Young Men,* and addressed it to all classes but "particularly the mercantile," that it was a waste of time and money, and if you were dancing you could not be attending to your business. While he does concede that it is a very good exercise, it still had best be left to the courtiers or gallants and not as an accomplishment for tradesmen.[23] Daniel C. Eddy classed dancing as a "Dangerous Amusement" and thought all who would partake of it would end in ruin.[24]

Nevertheless, the dancing masters were good businessmen in so far as they helped to create a demand for dance. The *American Journal of Education* for 1830 stated that while many parents felt it was a hardship to pay three dollars quarterly for instruction in the elementary branches of education, they did not mind paying three times as much for instruction in dancing. To prove its point the magazine gave some examples. There was a town where the schoolmaster received only five dollars and a half a month, and the people felt it was a hardship to pay him this; however the town did support two dancing schools that cost the residents at least a thousand dollars.[25] Horace Mann said much the same thing in a lecture in which he asked for greater compensation for school teachers.

In Philadelphia, the Reverend Andrew Law, professor of sacred music and president of the Harmonic Society, was forced to leave the city for the lack of encouragement. But the city was not too poor to reward the dancing masters amply.[26] F. Cuming tells that in his travel to the western country he met a Mr. Terasse who had

> no other resources left to gaine a provision for his family, but the teaching of the French language and dancing, in Lexington. The trustees of Transylvania College . . . employed him in the former, but had it not been for the latter, he might have starved. And here it may not be impertinent to remark, that in most parts of the United States, teachers of dancing meet with more encouragement than professors of any species of literary science.[27]

In this materialistic atmosphere, dancing not only helped one in business but also came to be recognized as a "good investment" in health and well-being. And when new educational theories in Europe began stressing exercise as a valuable part of education, the private dance teacher in America began to stress dance as a valuable and healthy exercise.

Francis Nichols, a Boston dancing master, felt that dancing not only kept the "body and limbs more active and more robust" but also tended "to regulate all our movements and restrain them within bounds of reason, decency and propriety." He thought dance was of particular benefit to men engaged in sedentary employment who had little chance for exercise.[28] W. P. Hazard, a Philadelphia dancing master, wrote that dance contributes much "to the preservation of health . . . and that children weak and feeble in limb will imperceptibly acquire a new vigor," while those persons who are already healthy and strong will retain their strength.[29] Charles Durang, son of the first American theatrical dancer, thought dance should be a part of physical education for children,[30] and D. L. Carpenter in *The Amateur's Preceptor on Dancing and Etiquette*, says, "Every child should learn fancy dances by themselves, if it is only for health. . . ."[31]

In the 1880's, both E. Woodworth Masters and Allen Dodworth thought that dancing should be taught in the public schools. "Dancing ought to form a part of physical education of children," wrote Masters, "and should be introduced into the public schools, not only for better health, but also to counteract the many improper attitudes and habits which they too often contact." [32] Dodworth suggested that dance

> would have a softening effect and produce a better result than sending the children into the yard or play-room for recreation, as it is called, which usually means to romp and practice rudeness, the strong abusing the weak, and all taking a daily lesson in tyranny, imposition, and turbulence the outcome of which is too often lawlessness in later life.[33]

The private dancing masters were not alone in their views on dance as a healthful exercise. Members of the medical profession also wrote of it as a promoter of health. The *Journal of Health*, in 1830 stated:

> We have said that dancing in moderation is a salutary exercise, but it is only when every limb and muscle is allowed to participate naturally and without constraint that the motion is thus communicated to the body. When on the contrary, dancing is performed in a dress by which this is prevented, to say nothing of the total absence of grace, injury, and that of a very serious character, is extremely liable to result.[34]

In an oration delivered before the Philadelphia Medical Society in 1831, Dr. Thomas Harris said, "Dancing is a most useful exercise, and not the less so for being agreeable." [35] Dr. John C. Warren, in a lecture delivered before the founding meeting of the American Institute of Instruction in 1830, stated that, "next to walking in the open air, the best exercise for a female is dancing." [36] At a convention of teachers in Lexington, Kentucky, Dr. Charles Caldwell, of Transylvania College, felt that "as an in-door exercise, for both males and females, nothing is superior to dancing." If some carry it to abuse, that is not a reason for discarding it for "Ten thousand people injure themselves by the abuse of eating, for one who does so, by that of dancing." [37]

III

Just as there were rapid changes and expansions in geographic, economic, and religious fields, so there were great strides made in public school education. From the beginning of the century to about 1820, there was little educational consciousness among the people as a whole; but a gradual awakening of such consciousness was being urged by private schools and societies and by the new ideas and reforms in education which were appearing in Europe.

With the advent of Jacksonian democracy and the rise of the common man, an even greater need for educating the people was evident. If the government of a democracy was to be in the hands of its citizens, it required an enlightened people. Also the rapid changes in science and economics caused a more complex society, which brought about a greater need for state support of education. In the latter half of the century, with education under the jurisdiction of the state, the state had authority to make some schooling compulsory; to make the schools free and supported by state taxes; to supervise and extend the system throughout the college level.[38]

To aid the adult in learning the arts and sciences, many organizations and institutions were established. Early in the century, there were the agricultural and mechanical institutions. In the 1830's the lyceum movement came to its height and lasted till the Civil War. In the eighties and nineties there was the establishment of the free-public-library movement and the Chautauqua movement. Magazine and the "penny press" also aided adult education. There were agricultural, political, scientific, literary, and religious magazines that told the latest methods and events on both sides of the Atlantic and Pacific oceans.

Toward the end of the century, there were magazines that dealt with dance and dance education. Two such magazines were *The Two Step* and *The Director*. *The Two Step* was started in 1894 and published monthly at Buffalo, New York. It dealt mainly with social dancing. *The Director* was published by Melvin Ballou Gilbert at Portsmouth, New Hampshire. It lasted only a year (December, 1897–98) but took in a wider range of dance activities than did *The Two Step*. It gave methods of teaching social dancing, lessons in esthetic dancing, news of dancing masters and dancing over the country, and included articles on physical education.

Emma Willard, Catherine Beecher and Mary Lyon crusaded for the cause of better education for women. Largely through the efforts of these pioneers in women's education, it was proved that the rigorous discipline that higher education required would not injure the health of girls and that they could study the same subjects that were offered to the boys both in the grammar schools and colleges. By the end of the century, many schools and colleges were open to both sexes.

During the first quarter of the century, dancing was still considered a very important part of education for the young. In 1803 *The Parents' Friend* was published and gave extracts from the principal works on education. It was aimed at aiding the parent in the education of his child. In the chapter on "Music, Singing, and Dancing" extracts were taken from Locke, Marquis Halifax, Burgh, Nelson, Chapone, and others.[39] As eighteenth century writers on education, they reflected their age in regard to the value of dance as a means of acquiring poise, manners and exercise. That such educational ideas were still in vogue in the early part of the century can be seen by Timothy Dwight's account of "Fashionable Education" in New England: "The children are solicitously taught music, dancing, embroidery, ease, confidence, graceful manners, &c., &c.," [40]

Samuel Goodrich, author of the Peter Parley books, feeling a need of disciplining his hands and feet and acquiring greater ease when entering into company, took lessons in dancing so that he might gain these things.[41] Edward Everett Hale and his brother were required to attend dancing school and while Edward Hale did not care for dancing, it was a part of "conventional civilization" and not left up to the children to decide.[42]

"Now let your boys and girls attend school," wrote Robert B. Thomas in *The Farmers' Almanack*. He warned parents to send their children to the town school rather than to the academies, because "fun, frolick, and filigree are too much practised at the academies for the benefit of a farmer's boy. Let them have a solid and useful education." [43] Thus Mr. Thomas states the growing attitude towards education in all ranks of life, both for boys and girls, and that is—it must be both *solid* and *useful*. It was for this reason, as well as for the growing interest in physical education, that dance was being stressed as a healthful and valuable form of exercise. It was on this basis that it gradually became a part of the school curriculum.

Despite Mr. Thomas' warning, dance by the middle of the century was invading the country school. The Reverend John L. Blake wrote in *The Farmer's Every-Day Book* that dance should be "in every country school." He believed that it should be under the direction of the schoolmaster.

> In the middle of the day, or prior to the commencement of the afternoon studies, let half an hour be spent in this fascinating exercise, as a reward of good conduct as scholars, and the prediction is made with confidence, that neither girls or boys will ever be tardy. Besides, it will refine the manners and the temper of the minds beyond calculation. Instead of diminishing progress in study, it will increase it. The design is by no means to fit them for the ballroom. It is simply to give them a healthful exercise; for boys, instead of playing ball—and the girls, instead of romping.[44]

The first book on gymnastics to be published in America, which attracted much attention at the time, was an English translation of Gutsmuth's *Gymnastics for the Young.* Published in 1802, the translator gave credit to Salzman for its authorship. Dancing was one of the exercises it strongly recommended because it tended to "unite gracefulness of motion with strength and agility." The type of dance that he recommends should be gymnastic in nature and fit for dancing in the open air. He would also have them accompanied by a song.[45]

Fifteen years later, dance was included in the program of the United States Military Academy at West Point. Baron Stauban had submitted a complete plan of the Academy to Washington in 1783 in which he had included dance in the course of instruction. However it was not until 1817 that the first class was started, and it was 1823 before it became an official course.

Pierre Thomas, the Academy's first sword master, was given permission to organize a voluntary dancing class for the cadets who had requested it. In 1823, Papanti, a famous Boston dancing master, was appointed instructor when dancing was made compulsory as a part of the summer encampment. Daily lessons of three-quarters of an hour were confined to the third and fourth class, and the period of instruction was from July 4 to August 28.[46]

After the founding of West Point, many military academies were soon to follow the same plan. Captain Alden Partridge, a graduate of West Point, founded the American Literary, Scientific and Military Academy in 1819, which was later to become Norwich University. The Military Department was founded on the same plan as that used at West Point, and was one of the first of many schools that were to follow. In 1826, P. Thomas, who had been West Point's first sword master and dancing instructor, was engaged for the same position at Captain Partridge's acamemy. Although dancing was offered to the students, it was not considered in the tuition of the regular studies, but could be had at five dollars per quarter. At the commencement exercises of 1824, a ball was given to conclude the events of the day and was so successful that it lasted till half-past three in the morning.[47] The American Institute, in Washington, D.C., also copied much of their program after West Point, and in the Military and Gymnastic Department they offered dancing as one of the exercises.[48]

The Round Hill School in Northampton, Massachusetts, is considered the birthplace of physical education in America. The school was opened in 1823 by Joseph Green Cogswell and George Bancroft. Both these men had traveled widely in Europe and had visited Fellenberg's school at Hofwyl; and used the European school as a model for theirs. One of the chief features of their school was the introduction of a definite system of physical training. Charles Beck, who had recently come from Germany, was engaged to teach the Jahn system of gymnastics. In 1826, instruction in dancing was added as a part of the curriculum. In an article about the school, the *Hampshire Gazette* stated that M. Guigon, from New York, had been engaged to instruct the dancing at the school. So that each person might receive three lessons a week, the school had been divided into fourteen classes. The classes were held after breakfast from half-past seven till nine.[49] To put their study of dancing into practice, balls and parties were a part of the social life of the school.

While dancing was regarded as a good form of exercise by some of the boys' schools, it was used to an even greater extent by the girls. Emma Willard, Catherine Beecher, and Mary Lyon believed that some form of physical education for girls was necessary. Mrs. Willard thought that dance should form that type of exercise used in schools for girls.

Mrs. Willard began her life work at the age of seventeen, when she started teaching in her home town of Berlin, Connecticut. Two years later, in 1806, she herself attended Mrs. Royse's school in Hartford, where French, drawing, needlework, and dancing were parts of the curriculum. The following year she became assistant teacher at the well-known Westfield Academy, at Westfield, Massachusetts. During the winter of 1807–8 she taught at Middlebury College. The winter was one of hardship because of the frequent storms and much snow and cold. However she wrote:

When it was so cold that we could live no longer I called all my girls on to the floor, and arranged them two and two in a long row for a country dance; and while those who could sing would strike up some stirring tune, I, with one of the girls for a partner would lead down the dance, and soon have them all in rapid motion. After which we went to our school exercises again.[50]

While at Middlebury she enjoyed the many parties and balls. It was at Middlebury that she met Doctor Willard, and in 1809 they were married. Although Mrs. Willard gave up teaching after her marriage, she returned to it again in 1814 because of her husband's financial difficulties. She opened her own school, which she called Middlebury Female Seminary. Here she worked on a plan for improving female education, which she finally entitled *An Address to the Public, Particularly to the Members of Legislature of New York, Proposing a Plan for the Improving of Female Education.* She sent a copy to DeWitt Clinton, then Governor of New York. Although the legislature did not pass it, the plan nevertheless caused an interest in the subject and much controversy both for and against higher education for women.

In the "Plan," Mrs. Willard describes what she considers the ideal course of study for a female seminary. She divided the course into four heads: Religious and Moral, Literary, Domestic, and Ornamental. Under Ornamental was "the grace of motion" and it was to be "learned chiefly from dancing." Besides giving a graceful carriage, it would form an exercise "needful to health and recreation" of youth. If such an exercise were forbidden the youth, they would seek it by sly methods which would lead them into many bad habits and evil ways. But if it were given after the confinement of the day and under the eyes of their instructor, it would have great value.

Dancing is exactly suited to this purpose, as also that of exercise; for perhaps in no other way, can so much healthy exercise be taken in so short a time. It has besides, this advantage over other amusements, that it affords nothing to excite the bad passions; but, on the contrary, its effects are, to soften the mind, to banish its animosities, and to open it to social impressions.[51]

For those that might object to dancing because it would keep the children from study, Mrs. Willard answered that balls would; but if dancing were to be practiced every day, by children of the same sex, without changing the place, the dress or the company, and under the guidance of those whom they are accustomed to obey, then it would become natural and no more emotion or excitement would be attached to it than to any other form of exercise or amusement.

In 1821, Mrs. Willard founded the Troy Female Seminary and put her "Plan" to work. The school was not only for the wealthy class, but for all classes. Many who could not pay the tuition but wanted to become teachers were given instruction which they afterwards repaid. In this school, the hour after six-o'clock supper was used for dancing, and as the girls went through the country dances, Mrs. Willard looked on and was more sure than ever that dance was a valuable exercise and recreation.

Two other women who were prominent in the field of education for women were Catherine Beecher and Mary Lyon. While neither believed that dance was the best form of exercise, the form of calisthenics they used resembled dance. Seven years after the opening of the Troy Female Seminary, Catherine Beecher founded the Hartford Female Seminary as an institution of higher learning for girls, and in 1832 she founded one in Cincinnati. In both of these she introduced a system of calisthenics which was based on dance. She says of her school in Cincinnati:

I invented a course of calisthenic exercises, accompanied by music, which was an improvement on the one I adopted at Hartford. The aim was to secure all the advantages supposed to be gained in dancing schools, with additional advantages for securing graceful movements to the sound of music.[52]

Despite the fact that she based much of her calisthenics on dance and dance movements, she writes in 1842 in *Domestic Economy* that she once held the opinion that dance was harmless and might be properly regulated. She allowed such a trial to be made by those who believed in dance, but results showed that no good effects came from dance that could not be gained in another way. At the time she was encouraged by the fact that while twenty-five years ago dancing was universally practiced, now it was almost impossible to get up a ball.[53] In 1856, she wrote in *Physiology and Calisthenics* that "there is one mode of *exercise* that is very common, and is earnestly defended on the grounds of its healthful tendencies, and that is *the dance*." She then agreed that if dance was practiced in the open air, in proper dress, and at proper times it would have no prejudices against it. However, like Mrs. Willard, she condemns balls.[54]

In her *Physiology and Calisthenics* the exercises she recommends for the feet are the five positions used in ballet. "The most important exercise for the feet are what are called the 'five positions.'" The reason for this was that it gave strength and elasticity to the feet and aided in the "preparation for easy and elegant walking." [55]

Mary Lyon, who opened the Mount Holyoke Seminary at South Hadley, Massachusetts, was the third of the three early pioneers in women's education. She believed that the physical education and exercise for girls should come from domestic duties and calisthenics. The first exercises were based on dance of the period and were designed for grace of motion.[56]

A book of exercises used at Mount Holyoke College was printed about 1853. The exercises consisted of such danc-like steps as double springs, skipping steps, and the "five positions," and were done to the singing of songs like *Lightly Row, What Fairy-like Music,* and *Haste Thee, Winter, Haste Away.*[57] In giving the exercises the teachers were cautioned in the *Book of Duties* that "care should be taken that the exercise does not become like dancing in the impression it makes on the observers."[58] This nevertheless was one of the reasons why the exercises were replaced in 1862 by the Dio Lewis system of exercises.

In other parts of the country, dance was also entering the schools. In 1827, the trustees of the Adams Academy proposed to have dance as a part of the curriculum for the following year. Zilpha P. Grant, who had been closely asso-ciated with Mary Lyon, was principal, but she refused the position for the following year because "one seventh of the study time was not devoted to the Bible." She opposed danc-ing on the grounds that there already was a systematic course and "all parents would not wish to have their children learn to dance."[59]

In Greenville, North Carolina, Mrs. Saffery adopted as her model "the celebrated system of Mrs. Willard." She announced that the polite arts of music, dancing and draw-ing would be a prominent feature in the school. Because some of the parents objected to dancing she also offered "a course in Calisthenics, calculated to promote a graceful carriage, a good walk, and a genteel address." This course of calisthenics was most likely based on dance.[60]

Almira Hart Lincoln Phelps, sister of Emma Willard, also did much for women's education. She followed her sister's system and, before opening her own school at Rahway and later at Patapsco, she taught at Troy. Both at Rahway and Patapsco she included dancing in the program. Mrs. Phelphs felt that dancing was of value for the effects it had on the motions and carriage of the body and because it aided cheerfulness and good humor.[61]

The girls at the Nashville Female Academy were not as fortunate as some when it came to dancing, although Dr. Elliott, a Methodist minister, introduced dancing in the Academy because he saw it as good exercise and recreation, and as conducive to good health and cheerfulness. Many of Dr. Elliott's colleagues did not approve of dancing in any form. Soon the controversy came to the attention of the *Nashville Christian Advocate,* whose editor, J. B. McFerrin, began an attack on Dr. Elliott for allowing dance to be taught in the gymnasium of the Nashville Female Academy. Although Dr. Elliott fought to prove that dancing was not sinful if taught as a recreation, McFerrin was too powerful and Elliott was ousted from both the school and the Methodist Church.[62]

While dance was accepted in a great number of the academies, it was not so readily accepted in the public-supported schools. Only when dance was presented as a form of exercise that required no extra preparation or attention was it received into the school system. Mr. Fowle introduced dance into the Female Monotorial School, at Boston, in this way.

In 1824, Mr. Fowle had introduced a regular and systematic physical education into his school, but because of misapprehension on the part of the parents it was discontinued. Still feeling that some form of calisthenics was necessary, he resorted to another bold measure and that was dance. According to the *American Journal of Education:*

One afternoon of every week was devoted to dancing. The instruction was given in the school-room, and Mr. Fowle was always present to preserve order. No extra dress was required, no exhibition balls and no association of the sexes were allowed. Indeed, all serious objections to this graceful art were removed, whilst great excellence was attained at comparatively little expense.[63]

In Cleveland in 1840, Jarvis F. Hanks petitioned the council to introduce music into the public schools. The council denied the request claiming that it was illegal to teach music in the schools. At the meeting, one of the councilmen said that if music was introduced dancing might also be introduced, but of the two he preferred dancing.[64] In 1855, the council made an effort to do away with the rule that allowed the students to leave school to attend lessons in music and dancing and other lessons. The rule allowing them to leave school had been of such long standing that a way was worked out that allowed them to continue the practice.[65]

In 1894, the Methodist ministers objected to dancing in the Cleveland high schools and "thereby reopened a debate that had waxed warm in former years." The school officials stated that their reasons for allowing dance was that it was a healthful recreation; and because they did not allow the sexes to dance together, and the dancing was confined to the lunch period, it was of value in keeping the children in school and off the streets. From the parents there had been no complaints. On special occasions the senior girls did hold class parties in the school where the sexes danced together, but they were well supervised by the teachers and this was better than sending them to a hired hall.[66]

The infant school, which was for children four years of age, was imported from England early in the century. While the idea was popular at the time and lasted several years, it was replaced by the kindergarten. The kindergarten was founded in Germany by Friedrich Froebel with the idea that there should be directed self-activity and the process of learning by doing. To attain this goal he believed in learning through play, song, gesture and self-expression. Much of the activity was of a dancelike nature.

Francis W. Parker, the pioneer of progressive education and the principal of the Cook County School in Chicago, based much of his work on the Froebelian principle of self-expression. Many of his ideas of expression came from the work of Delsarte, which was also very popular at the time.[67] Parker, a great believer in rhythm and self-expression, allowed the children to express themselves through movement however and whenever they desired. Thus Parker and his associates introduced a crude form of expressive dance. Parker's idea of self-expression which allowed the children to speak through any medium was not accepted by the authoritative school of thought which believed that "children should be seen and not heard." Thus the idea of speaking through rhythm and physical movement was considered silly and outrageous. Because of such attitudes on the part of the schools of the day, the dance as a creative form of expression had to wait till the twentieth century.[68]

While dance was slowly becoming a part of the curriculum in the secondary schools and academies, it was only in the latter part of the century that colleges and universities offered it as a course of instruction. The early colleges, being founded by church denominations, had as their purpose the education of a ministry. Slowly, and only as the state-controlled colleges came into existence and the curriculum began to change to more specialized and functional courses, did dance appear to any great degree.

The early laws of some of the colleges forbade the students to attend dances or dancing schools. The pupils of Queen's College (Rutgers) in 1810 were forbidden to "attend any dancing assembly or dancing school or fencing master in the city of New Brunswick." [69] Dance was against the rules at Guilford College in North Carolina, but the students danced, and if they were quick enough to run at the sound of their professor's footsteps, they were not caught. However, if they were caught, it was suggested by one person that they could say they were taking personal exercises. [70]

The University of North Carolina feeling that a university should be quiet and a place of study made a rule whereby "no shouting, whistling, dancing, or boisterous noise shall be permitted in the passages or rooms of the College at any time. . . ." [71] Some of the colleges saw no harm in dance and permitted the students to attend dancing schools if the college did not provide such a course. Harvard had licensed a dancing school by 1815. [72] Jefferson suggested that dance be included in the curriculum at the University of Virginia because it was one of the arts that "embellished life." [73] St. Mary's College, in Baltimore, offered dance to its students. [74] At the University of Georgia dance was not allowed under the presidency of Wadell; but after his departure, that rule changed as students went to both dances and dancing schools. [75]

Many of the colleges that had allowed dancing in their early history placed a ban on it by the thirties. Whereas some of the colleges forbade the students to attend dancing schools or dances outside the college they held their own commencement hops, proms or balls, and the event soon became the long-awaited incident in the social life of the college student. The college laws of 1848 at the University of South Carolina stated that "no student, or students, shall be permitted to make any ball or festive entertainment except a ball at Commencement. . . ."[76] By 1838, Class Day at Harvard had become such a wild affair that President Quincy warned the students to abstain from punch and dancing. The affair soon became so dull that both were allowed once again.[77] President Johnson, of Louisiana State University, announced in 1882, that the "hops or dancing parties" which had been held during the past years would no longer be permitted. However, due to the opposition aroused, he did permit the commencement hop.[78]

While sporadic attempts were made to introduce dance into the schools and colleges it was not until the revival of interest in physical education and exercise, just before and at the close of the Civil War, that any real gains were made. It was between the period of the Civil War and the close of the century that dance was to become an integral part of physical education and thus a part of the school program. Because dance was to enter the school program through the door of physical education its history follows closely the history of physical education of the period.

In 1880, Dio Lewis brought before the American Institute of Education a system of "new gymnastics" which was demonstrated by trained pupils. His system was so well received that in 1861 he opened the Boston Normal Institute of Physical Education, and it was here he worked on perfecting his system. Then in 1862 the developed system was published in a volume called *The New Gymnastics for Men, Women and Children.*[79]

While Lewis states in the preface of his book that the "exercises are arranged to music and are found to possess a charm superior to that of dancing and other social amusements,"[80] many of his free gymnastics still resemble a modified form of dance. In his marching, leaping, and skipping exercises, many of the figures used are the same as those used in folk dancing. Two of the exercises under skipping were as follows:

No. 4. Skip through the whole length of the hall with a Chassez step.

No. 9. Again, skip down through the hall, joining only the right hand with your partner. This may be pleasantly varied by one of the parties whirling as you go, allowing his hand to turn in the hand of the partner.[81]

Lewis was of the opinion that his exercises were superior to dance because they brought into play the whole body, where dance brought into play only the legs. However, in his school for girls which he opened in 1864 at Lexington, Massachusetts, dancing played a part. He says of the exercises at the school, "They exercised twice a day, half an hour, in gymnastic exercises and danced an hour about three times a week."[82]

Catherine Beecher had used music with her calisthenics but it was Dio Lewis who helped popularize its use. He suggested that a small drum may be used to keep time with, and at times had advantage over other instruments in that "it secured more perfect consort" than any other instrument.

Lewis' gymnastics became very popular and were used in many of the secondary schools and colleges over the country. Their value lay in the fact that through the use of free exercises no extra equipment or room was necessary and therefore they could be done in the school room.

The prospectus and first catalogue of Vassar College stated that physical education would form a part of the courses of the school and that the Dio Lewis system of light gymnastics would be used.[83]

Many of the citizens posed quite a problem for the lady principal when they urged her to have dancing taught at Vassar. The liberal attitude taken in this direction is shown by the communication from the founder, Matthew Vassar, to the Board of Trustees.

> Among other physical exercises claiming consideration, dancing has been presented to our Executive Committee for consideration, and has been urged by many citizens. The attention in the Christian community has been awakened by recent writings pro and con on these questions. . . . Years ago I made up my judgment on these great questions in the religious point of view, and came to the decision favorable to amusements. I have never practiced public dancing in my life, and yet in view of its being a healthful and graceful exercise, I heartily approve of it, and now recommend it being taught in the College to all pupils whose parents or guardians desire it.[84]

From the time of Lewis to the end of the century there was a greater interest in rhythmical gymnastics and many of the activities began to take on a dancelike nature. There was a greater interest in gracefulness, ease of movement and carriage of the body. The roundel had been introduced into the German system by Adolph Spiess, and while it was devised for the children to be used in the schools, turnhalls, and the playgrounds it was used to some extent by the women. It was based on folk songs and consisted of marching, skipping, and running movements.[85]

Musical drills also became very popular, with their various types of marching and "broom drills." They quite often included dance steps such as follow-stepping, catch-stepping and the chassez. It was in this period that the

Delsarte System of Exercise became popular and had a great influence on the modern dance movement which was to appear at the turn of the century.

François Delsarte, born in Solesme, France, studied to be a singer and actor, but due to the misfortune of having studied with incompetent teachers his voice was ruined and he gave up the idea of a singing career. He then began to study and formulate the laws of expression.[86]

Delsarte, himself, never devised any system of gymnastics. "Delsarte esthetic gymnastics is purely an American idea,"[87] wrote Genevieve Stebbins, who did much to propagate the Delsarte System. It was the uninformed instructors who had little or no idea of the philosophy of Delsarte that caused the Delsarte System to become known as the "doctrine of Limpness."[88] The system was based on exercises that stressed relaxation. "Americanized Delsarte Culture teaches as well as preaches the 'gospel of relaxation,'"[89] wrote Emily M. Bishop, instructor of Delsarte Culture at the Chautauqua Institute. It also stressed the use of statue-posing and tableaux-making that purported to show the various emotions. It was often used in connection with the recitation of a poem or the singing of a song.

William G. Anderson, described below, seems to have had the Delsarte System in mind when he suggests in his book *Light Gymnastics* that the attitudes of such famous statues as the Apollo Belvedere and Discobolus Athlete could be used for boys and young men. These positions and attitudes were always accompanied by appropriate music.[90] The Delsarte System with all its statue-building and posing included a great many dance movements and maneuvers which were to hasten the day for dance as a part of the school curriculum.

In 1887, Dr. William G. Anderson, Director of the

Brooklyn Normal School of Gymnastics, began to use dance as a part of his program. Dr. Anderson, born in St. Joseph, Michigan, in 1860, became a champion of gymnastics early in life. While attending school in Boston he became a pupil of Robert J. Roberts at the Boston Young Men's Christian Association and was later to become the superintendent of the Cleveland, Ohio, Young Men's Christian Association gymnasium. While in Cleveland, he received his degree of Doctor of Medicine from the Cleveland Medical College.

In 1885 he decided to make physical education his life work and in that year accepted an appointment at Adelphi Academy as director of the gymnasium. It was here that he organized the Brooklyn Normal School of Physical Education. In 1892 he moved to New Haven to become associate director of the Yale University gymnasium. Dr. Anderson was asked in 1886 to take charge of the summer school at the Chautauqua Institute.[91]

In writing about the first year at the Brooklyn Normal School of Gymnastics, Anderson said:

> I felt that dancing could be used to arouse greater interest in Gymnastics. I also felt that the right kind of dancing would develop the heart, as well as add to the grace of my students.[92]

The first dance he taught was a "straight jig"; but in succeeding years he studied Russian ballet, clog, reels, and various other types and forms of dance, and all of these he taught at Brooklyn, Chautauqua, and Yale.[93]

It was also in 1887 that Dr. Dudley A. Sargent started the Harvard Summer School of Physical Training. Dr. Sargent, born in Belfast, Maine, in 1849, became interested in physical education when, at the age of fifteen, he witnessed a circus performance, and later on, when he saw gymnastic exhibitions given by Bowdoin College students. His great interest in and practice of gymnastics won him an engagement with a circus, and in 1869 he became director of the gymnasium at Bowdoin College.

In 1875 Dr. Sargent secured a job as instructor of gymnastics at Yale and at the same time entered the Medical School. In 1879, he was appointed by Harvard University as assistant professor of physical training and director of Hemenway Gymnasium. In 1881, he organized the Sanatory Gymnasium in Boston which later became the Sargent School of Physical Education.[94]

As the need for physical education teachers became greater, Dr. Sargent started the summer school at Harvard and asked Christian Eberhard to teach dance. Mr. Eberhard realized the value of dance, but knew also that the church frowned upon it, and so the term "Fancy Step" was used for the want of a better one.[95] He taught such steps as the change step, Schottisch step, touch step, waltz, and mazurka steps.[96] The program for Visitors' Day in 1892 shows that one of the events was "Dancing and Running Maze," and that Mr. Eberhard was the instructor of the event.[97]

In 1894, Dr. Sargent introduced a new type of calisthenics, called "Aesthetic Calisthenics," at both the Harvard Summer School and the Sargent School. This new system had been developed by Melvin Ballou Gilbert, a Portland dance teacher, who had his own gymnasium for women. Gilbert developed his system from ballet. He realized that the regular gymnastic work was not the best physical training for women, and that strict ballet was not suited to all women, from a biological standpoint.[98]

The system he devised goes by various names—Gilbert, Aesthetic and Classic. According to Gilbert it consists of the long-established five positions of the feet and the five positions of the arms, together with the positions of the whole body known as attitudes, arabesques, poses, elevations, groupings, etc. From these precepts are established, whereby the steps, attitudes and motions are systematic and in strict harmony with time and music.[99]

One of the principal reasons that Dr. Sargent introduced dancing into the gymnasium program was that through the use of rhythmic exercise it gave a "means of attaining grace, suppleness and easy carriage" that was not found in the gymnastic exercises as they were practiced.[100] In the announcement of the summer course for 1894 the course was called "Calisthenics" and was described as "light and simple rhythmic movements of body and limbs for the cultivation of grace and elegance in form and bearing, figure marching and dancing steps." In the catalogue for the same year Gilbert had the title of Special Instructor in Aesthetic Calisthenics, whereas the next year lists him as Instructor of Dancing Calisthenics.[101]

Carl Schrader in writing about the activities of the Hemenway Gymnasium states that—

> Dr. Sargent was a fearless pioneer and dared to stress dancing as an important and integral adjunct to physical education. Gilbert was the man whom Dr. Sargent intrusted with this innovation. It was a great success from the beginning and the Gilbert School in Boston was the first mecca to which women flocked to learn the new art.[102]

The men were taught by Oliver Hebbert, who according to Schrader "may well be considered the pioneer in dancing for men."

As originally designed, the course in "dancing calisthenics" was for both men and women, but as Dr. Sargent wrote later, the exercises became so esthetic that the boys would not take the classes and then "it became necessary to modify the dancing so as to give more opportunity for a heavier kind of work." [103] Therefore, the course's original intentions had to wait for someone else to design a dance course of a masculine type that boys would accept.

Dr. Sargent's ideas on physical education and dance fitted well into Harvard's new program of education. President Eliot had inaugurated a new plan of general education at Harvard which did away with the rigid curriculum of the old classical education by expanding its program of studies and making courses elective. Dr. Eliot saw dance as a valuable part of education, for in a letter to Charles Francis Adams he wrote:

> I have often said that if I were compelled to have one required subject in Harvard College, I would make it dancing if I could. West Point has been very wise in this respect, and I am inclined to think that Annapolis has had the same policy.[104]

He considered dancing, as did Hazlitt, that "'these are the small coins in the intercourse of life.'"

Dr. Sargent's introduction of dancing calisthenics into the school program was a great innovation. It was the first time that a definite system of dance was taught in the schools, and it was also a break from the social and folk forms that had previously been taught. It was at this point that dance became an integral part of physical education and thus a part of the school and college program. Dr. Sargent's system was used widely throughout the country as many teachers studied with him at Harvard.

Postscript

This is the background from which suddenly emerged the dance as an art form which in the twentieth century brought dance to its highest expression as an educational experience.

This is the background upon which Gertrude Colby built her Natural Dance movement in 1914. Colby, a student of Gilbert, found while teaching at the Speyer School that her early training was too formal for children. In looking for some freer form of dance that would aid her, she studied with Chalif and those who taught the Delsarte and Dalcroze methods. She found that her real inspiration came from the work of Isadora Duncan, who had revolted against the formal forms when she made her debut in 1895. From that inspiration Colby developed what she called Natural Dance.

Margaret H'Doubler, who had come to New York from Wisconsin to find some form of dance to take the place of the more formal types that were being taught, came into contact with Gertrude Colby and Bird Larson. Although the work of Colby and Larson did not satisfy her, it did give her a glimpse of what to look for and what not to do. She then continued her research and in 1917 returned to Wisconsin to teach a truly educational dance form. She was more interested in what dance would do for the student personally than dance from a theatrical standpoint.

Another of Gilbert's students was Elizabeth Burchenal, who after graduating from his school taught his method.

Her interest gradually turned to folk dance. In 1905 she was asked by Luther Gulick to take charge of the newly formed folk-dance movement of the New York City Public Schools. She accepted the offer, and it was largely due to her pioneering efforts in the folk-dance movement that folk dance has grown to its importance today.

Mary Wood Hinman, another ardent follower and supporter of folk dance, had studied with Gilbert and taught his method. Her interest turned to clog and folk dance and it is in this field that she is best known.

Just as Isadora Duncan had felt the influence of Delsarte, so had Ruth St. Denis. While Ruth St. Denis turned to the oriental forms, she too was interested in freeing dance from its many formalities. In 1914 she met Ted Shawn and out of this union came the Denishawn School. The Denishawn School, through its many tours over the country and its schools in several of the large cities, carried dance to all parts of the United States. While some of its pupils, like Martha Graham, Doris Humphrey, and Charles Weidman are better known, it was the great number of public-school teachers that studied at the Denishawn School who carried the message of dance and dance education to the remote schools over the length and breadth of the country.

Ted Shawn in his book on Delsarte shows how the modern dance as we know it today was greatly influenced and benefited by the work of Delsarte. Shawn himself, having studied the laws of Delsarte and adapting them to dance, not only aided dance by his partnership in the Denishawn School but in 1933, after teaching at Springfield College, formed an all-male dance company. As his all-male company toured the many colleges and universities throughout the country, they aided the cause of dance education for men.

These are but a few of the many dance teachers that built upon and benefited by the pioneering work of those now almost forgotten men and women who did so much for dance education. And, just as they built upon the dance education of the past generations, so will future generations build upon the present.

Bibliographical Notes

PART ONE

Dance Education in the Seventeenth Century

1. Perry Miller and Thomas H. Johnson: *The Puritans* (New York: American Book Company; 1938), p. 43.

2. Thomas J. Wertenbaker: *The First Americans* (New York: The Macmillan Company; 1927), p. 113.

3. Percy A. Scholes: *The Puritans and Music in England and New England* (London: Oxford University Press; 1934).

4. "Letter of John Cotton to R. Levitt," *Collections*, Massachusetts Historical Society; Series 2, Vol. X (1823), pp. 183–84.

5. Allen Johnson and Dumas Malone (eds.): *Dictionary of American Biography* (New York: Charles Scribner's Sons; 1930), Vol. IV, p. 461.

6. William Bradford: *Bradford's History of "Plimoth Plantation"* (Boston: Wright & Potter Printing Company; 1898), pp. 285–88.

7. "Diary of Samuel Sewall," *Collections*, Massachusetts Historical Society, Series 5, Vol. V, p. 178.

8. Nathaniel B. Shurtleff (ed.): *Records of the Governor and Company of the Massachusetts Bay in New England* (Boston: 1853–54), Vol. I, p. 233.

9. Nathaniel B. Shurtleff and others (compilers): *Records of the Colony of New Plymouth in New England* [1620–1692] (Boston: 1855–61), Vol. II, p. 174.

10. F. B. Dexter (ed.): *Ancient Town Records: New Haven Town Records 1649–1684* (New Haven: New Haven Colony Historical Society; 1917–19), Vol. II, pp. 23–25.

11. Shurtleff, *Records . . . Massachusetts*, Vol. I, p. 233.

12. John Locke: *Some Thoughts Concerning Education,* edited by Robert H. Quick (Cambridge University Press; 1880), pp. 174, 42–43.

13. Charles Morton: *Compendium Physicae* (The Colonial Society of Massachusetts; 1940), Vol. XXXIII, p. 191.

14. D. N. Kennedy: *English Dances No. 1: Country Dances —Playford* (London: The English Folk and Song Society; n.d.), p. 1.

15. John Playford: *The English Dancing Master, reprinted from the first edition of 1650,* edited by Leslie Bridgewater and Hugh Mellor (London: Hugh Mellor; 1933), p. iii.

16. S. Foster Damon: "The History of Square-Dancing," *Proceedings,* American Antiquarian Society, April, 1952, p. 66.

17. Carl Bridenbaugh: *Cities in the Wilderness* (New York: The Ronald Press Company; 1938), pp. 117–18.

18. *Records of the Court of Assistants of the Colony of the Massachusetts Bay, 1630–1692.* (Boston: 1901), Vol. I, p. 197.

19. "Diary of Samuel Sewall," pp. 103–4.

20. *Ibid.,* pp. 121, 145.

21. [Increase Mather]: *An Arrow Against Profane and Promiscuous Dancing: Drawn out of the Quiver of the Scriptures, By the Ministers of Christ at Boston in New-England* (Boston: Samuel Green; 1684), p. 1.

22. *Ibid.,* p. 2.

23. *Ibid.,* p. 24.

24. [Cotton Mather]: *A Cloud of Witnesses* (Boston: B. Green & J. Allen [?]; 1700[?]), p. 1. In Yale University Library.

25. *Ibid.,* p. 4.

26. Clark Wessler, Constance L. Skinner, William Wood: *Adventure in the Wilderness* (New Haven: Yale University Press; 1909), Vol. I, p. 462.

27. Mrs. Schuyler Van Rensselaer: *History of the City of New York in the Seventeenth Century* (New York: The Macmillan Company; 1909), Vol. I, p. 462.

28. John R. Brodhead: *History of the State of New York* (New York: Harper & Brothers; 1871), Vol. II, p. 465.

29. Lewis B. Wright: *The First Gentlemen of Virginia* (San Marino: The Huntington Library; 1940), p. 39.

30. Cornelius J. Heatwole: *A History of Education in Virginia* (New York: The Macmillan Company; 1916), Chap. V.

31. *Ibid.*, pp. 28–29.

32. Philip A. Bruce: *Social Life in Virginia in the Seventeenth Century*, 2d ed. (Lynchburg: J. P. Bell Company; 1927), p. 189.

33. *Ibid.*, pp. 187–88.

34. *Ibid.*, p. 257.

35. *Ibid.*, p. 186.

36. Dauphin of Durand: *A Huguenot's Exile in Virginia, or Voyages of a Frenchman exiled for his Religion, with a description of Virginia & Maryland: From the Hague Edition of 1687*, intro. and notes by Gilbert Chinard (New York: The Press of the Pioneers, Inc.; 1934), p. 158.

37. Bruce, *op. cit.*, pp. 189–90.

38. Richard Brathwaite: *The English Gentleman*, 2d ed. (London: Felix Kyngston; 1633), pp. 204–5.

39. Richard Brathwaite: *The English Gentlewoman.* (London: B. Alsop & T. Fawcet; 1631), pp. 76–77.

40. Lord Marquess of Halifax: "The Lady's New Year's Gift: or Advice to a Daughter," *Miscellanies* (London: Matt. Gillyflouer; 1700), p. 83.

PART TWO

Dance Education in the Eighteenth Century

1. *The Monthly Magazine and American Review* (New York: T. & J. Swords), Vol. II, No. 1 (Jan., 1800), pp. 14–15.

2. Robert Francis Seybolt: *Source Studies in American Colonial Education: The Private School*, University of Illinois, College of Education, Bureau of Educational Research, Bulletin No. 28, pp. 100–02.

3. Rutherford Goodwin: *A Brief & True Report Concerning Williamsburg in Virginia* (Williamsburg: Colonial Williamsburg, Inc.; 1941), pp. 25, 184–86.

4. *South Carolina Gazette*, Feb. 15, 1735; Dec. 4, 1737. Quoted in Hennig Cohen: *The South Carolina Gazette, 1732–1775* (Columbia: The University of South Carolina; 1953), p. 116.

5. James Truslow Adams: *The Provincial Society, 1690–1763* (New York: The Macmillan Company; 1943), pp. 275–77.

6. William Warren Sweet: *Religion in Colonial America* (New York: Charles Scribner's Sons; 1947), Chap. IX.

7. Cotton Mather: *Magnalia Christi Americana* (Hartford: Silas Anderus; 1820), Vol. II, p. 276.

8. Cotton Mather: "Diary," Collections, Massachusetts Historical Society, 7th series, Vol. VIII, pp. 146–47.

9. *Boston Gazette*, Nov. 20, 1732. Quoted in George F. Dow: *Arts and Crafts in New England, 1704–1775.* (Topsfield: The Wayside Press; 1927), pp. 9–11.

10. James Mulhern: *A History of Secondary Education in Pennsylvania* (Philadelphia: By the Author; 1933), p. 159.

11. *Philadelphia Minerva*, Vol. II, No. 97 (Dec. 10, 1796).

12. *Philadelphia Minerva*, Vol. II, No. 98 (Dec. 17, 1796).

13. *Loc. cit.*

14. C. G. Chamberlayne (ed.): *The Vestry Book and Register of St. Peter's Parish, New Kent and James City Counties, Va., 1684–1786* (Richmond: 1937), p. 665.

15. Alonzo Willard Fortune: *The Disciples in Kentucky* (The Convention of the Christian Churches in Kentucky; 1932), p. 28.

16. Henry Howe: *Historical Collections of the Great West* (Cincinnati: Henry Howe; 1854), pp. 88–91.

17. E. D. Andrews: "The Dance in Shaker Ritual." In Paul Magriel (ed): *Chronicles of the American Dance* (New York: Henry Holt & Company; 1948), pp. 3–5.

18. *The Acts and Resolves, Public and Private, of the Province of Massachusetts Bay* (Boston: Rand, Avery & Co.; 1881), Vol. I, Province Laws, 1711–1712, 6th sess., Sect. 8, p. 680.

19. *Ibid.*, Sect. 13, p. 681.

20. *Ibid.*, Vol. IV, Province Laws, 1760–61, 3rd sess., Sect. 9, p. 417.

21. *Journal of Congress*, Oct. 20, 1774, Vol. I, p. 78.

22. Charles H. Sherrill: *French Memories of Eighteenth-Century America* (New York: Charles Scribner's Sons; 1915), p. 36.

23. Evangeline W. and Charles M. Andrews (eds.): *Journal of a Lady of Quality* (New Haven: Yale University Press; 1922), p. 149.

24. Henry M. Brooks (ed.): *Quaint and Curious Advertisements* (Boston: Tichnor & Company; 1886), p. 2.

25. Edwin G. Dexter: *The History of Education in the United States* (New York: The Macmillan Co.; 1904), p. 66.

26. *Rivington's New York Gazetteer*, Feb. 24, 1774. Quoted in Seybolt, *op. cit.*, pp. 96–98.

27. *Collections*, Massachusetts Historical Society, 6th series, Vol. IV, p. 223.

28. Charles Francis Adams: *Familiar Letters of John Adams and his wife Abigail Adams, during the Revolution.* (New York: Hurst & Houghton; 1876), p. xi.

29. Seybolt, *op. cit.*, pp. 69–82.

30. *Boston News-Letter*, Mar. 2–9, 1712. Quoted in Seybolt, *op cit.*, pp. 74–75.

31. *Boston Gazette*, Jan. 16–23, 1738. Quoted in Dow, *op. cit.*, p. 12.

32. *The Virginia Gazette* (Dixon & Hunter), No. 1324 (Dec. 20, 1776), p. 4.

33. *South Carolina Gazette*, Aug. 6, 1741. Cited in Julia Cherry Spurill: *Woman's Life and Work in the Southern Colonies* (Chapel Hill: University of North Carolina Press; 1938), p. 198.

34. *South Carolina Gazette*, May 17, 1770. Cited in Spurill, *op. cit.*, p. 199.

35. *The Kentucky Gazette* (Bradford), June 6, 1789.

36. *Boston News-Letter,* April 1716. Cited in Scholes, *op cit.,* pp. 36–37.

37. James Duncan Phillips: *Salem in the Eighteenth Century* (Boston: Houghton Mifflin Company; 1937), p. 182.

38. *Hampshire and Berkshire Chronicle* (Springfield, Mass.), Feb. 12, 1793.

39. *The New York Gazette,* Sept. 24, 1759; Oct. 15, 1770. Quoted in *The Arts and Crafts in New York, 1726–1776; Collections,* New York Historical Society (1938), p. 368, 369.

40. *Pennsylvania Mercury,* No. 465 (Nov. 28, 1728); No. 500 (Aug. 7, 1729). Cited in Anna J. DeArmond; *Andrew Bradford, Colonial Journalist* (Newark: University of Delaware; 1949), p. 156.

41. *Pennsylvania Mercury,* No. 1019 (July 12, 1739). Cited in DeArmond, *op. cit.,* p. 156.

42. Raymond W. Albright: *Two Centuries of Reading, Pa.* (Reading: Historical Society of Berks County; 1948), p. 128.

43. *Virginia Gazette* (Dixon & Hunter), No. 1254 (Aug. 19, 1775), p. 3.

44. *The Kentucky Gazette,* Mar. 22, 1788, p. 1.

45. *The South Carolina Gazette,* May 27, 1732; April 24, 1749; Aug. 7, 1749; Dec. 11, 1749. Cited in Cohen, *op. cit.,* p. 33.

46. *Georgia Gazette,* Aug. 30, 1764. Cited in Elbert W. G. Boogher: *Secondary Education in Georgia, 1732–1858* (Philadelphia: University of Pennsylvania; 1933), p. 135.

47. *Boston News-Letter,* Feb. 23, 1712; *Boston Weekly Rehearsal,* Aug. 19, 1734; *New York Gazette,* June 14, 1731; *Pennsylvania Mercury,* Mar. 14, 1727/28; Mar. 18, 1730/31; Dec. 30, 1735; *South Carolina Gazette,* Sept. 10, 1744.

48. *Kentucky Gazette,* July 11, 1798.

49. John Roger Williams (ed.): *Philip Vickers Fithian Journal and Letters, 1767–1774.* (Princeton: Princeton Historical Association; 1900), p. 64.

50. John C. Fitzpatrick (ed.): *The Diaries of George Washington, 1748–1774* (Boston: Houghton Mifflin Co.; 1925), Vol. I, pp. 373, 397.

51. *Virginia Gazette* (Dixion & Hunter), Oct. 14, 1775.

52. *Virginia Gazette* (Parks), April 13, 1739.

53. *Virginia Gazette* (Parks), Aug. 17, 1739.

54. *Virginia Gazette* (Purdie, Dixion), April 17, 1771.

55. Harry Toulmin: *The Western Country in 1793, Reports on Kentucky and Virginia,* edited by Marion Tinling and Godfrey Davis (San Marino: The Huntington Library; 1948), p. 66.

56. *Mirror* (Washington, Ky.), Oct. 16, 1799.

57. *Providence Gazette and Country Journal,* Jan. 15, 22, 29, Feb. 5, 12, 19, 1763. In Connecticut Historical Society.

58. *William and Mary College Quarterly Magazine,* 1st series, Vol. V, No. 1, p. 66.

59. Williams, *op. cit.,* p. 226.

60. William B. Parker and Jonas Viles: *Thomas Jefferson, Letters and Addresses* (New York: Sun Dial Press; 1908), p. 32.

61. George Francis Dow: *The Holyoke Diaries, 1709–1856* (Salem: The Essex Institute; 1911), p. 7.

62. *Boston Evening Post,* Dec. 10, 1744. Quoted in Thomas Woody: *A History of Women's Education in the United States* (New York: The Science Press; 1929), Vol. I, pp. 130–31.

63. For a more comprehensive account of the educational books used during the period see John E. Mason: *Gentlefolk in the Making,* Chap. IV, V, VII, and Spurill, *op. cit.,* Chap. X.

64. William Darrill: *The Gentleman Instructed.* 6th ed. (London: 1716), p. 20.

65. *The Ladies Library, Written by a Lady and Published by Sir Richard Steele,* 4th ed. (London: 1732), Vol. II, p. 41.

66. Lady Sarah Pennington: "An Unfortunate Mother's Advice to Her Absent Daughters; in a Letter to Miss Pennington," *The Literary Miscellany* (London: 1804), Vol. VI, pp. 14, 28.

67. Dr. Gregory: *A Father's Legacy to His Daughters* (Boston: 1794), p. 107.

68. James Fordyce: *Sermons to Young Women,* 14th ed. (London: C. Baldwin, 1814), Vol. I, pp. 181–84.

69. *Sentimental Beauties, and Moral Delineations from the Celebrated Dr. Blair, and much Admired Authors; Selected with a View to Refine the Taste, Rectify the Judgement; and mould the Heart to Virtue,* 4th ed. (Philadelphia: F. Baily; 1792), p. 52.

70. *Principles of Politeness, and of Knowing the World, by the Late Lord Chesterfield. Methodised and digested under distinct Heads, with additions by the Rev. Dr. John Trusler* (Boston: 1794), pp. 20, 22.

71. *William and Mary College Quarterly Magazine,* 1st series, Vol. III, No. 4 (April 1895), p. 251.

72. *The South Carolina Gazette,* Dec. 6, 1751. Cohen, *op. cit.,* p. 135.

73. *Virginia Magazine of History,* Vol. III, No. 4 (April 1896), p. 391.

74. Pierre Rameau: *The Dancing Master,* trans. by C. W. Beaumont (London: C. W. Beaumont; 1931), pp. vii–viii.

75. *Ibid.,* pp. 1–2

76. *Ibid.,* p. 5 ff.

77. *Ibid.,* p. 13 ff.

78. *Ibid.,* pp. 113–14.

79. Sherrill, *op. cit.,* p. 31.

80. Williams, *op. cit.,* p. 226.

81. *Huntington Papers,* Connecticut Historical Society, Vol. XX (1923), p. 462.

82. *Pennsylvania Mercury,* Aug. 31, 1738.

83. *American Journal of Education,* New series, Vol. I (1830), p. 442.

84. Caleb Bingham: *The Columbian Orator* (Boston: Manning and Loring; n.d.), p. 191–92.

85. Caleb Bingham: *The American Preceptor,* 10th ed. (Boston: Manning and Loring; 1801), pp. 140–41.

86. "Importance of Female Education—and of education of young men in their Native country, addressed to every American," *American Magazine* (Noah Webster), May, 1788, pp. 339–40.

87. *Ibid.*, p. 371.

88. *Ibid.*, p. 369.

89. Emily Ellsworth F. Ford: *Notes on the Life of Noah Webster* (New York: Privately Printed; 1912), Vol. I, p. 226.

90. Benjamin Rush: *Sermons to the Rich and Studious on Temperance and Exercise* (London: Reprinted by T. Collier; 1772), pp. 48–49.

91. *The New England Courant,* No. 4 (May 7, 1722). In Albert Henry Smyth: *The Writings of Benjamin Franklin* (New York: The Macmillan Company; 1907), Vol. II, pp. 14–15.

92. Benjamin Peirce: *A History of Harvard University, from its Foundation, in the Year 1636, to the Period of the American Revolution* (Cambridge: Brown, Shattuck & Company; 1833), pp. 161–62.

93. *Collections,* Colonial Society of Massachusetts, Vol. XXXI (1935), p. 382.

94. Charles Francis Adams (ed.): *The Works of John Adams, Second President of the United States* (Boston: Charles Little & James Brown; 1850), Vol. II, pp. 288–89.

95. Thomas Jefferson Wertenbaker: *Princeton, 1746–1796.* (Princeton: Princeton University Press; 1946), p. 39.

96. Princeton Library Mss., AM. 11288; also in Wertenbaker.

97. Wertenbaker, *op. cit.,* p. 77.

98. Williams, *op. cit.,* pp. 287, 290.

99. Charles F. Thwing: *A History of Higher Education in America* (New York: D. Appleton & Company; 1906), p. 145.

100. Franklin B. Dexter (ed.): *Literary Diary of Ezra Stiles* (New York: 1901), Vol. III, pp. 10–11, 15.

101. Thwing, *op. cit.,* p. 145.

102. J. Bennett Nolan: *The Only Franklin in Franklin's College* (Philadelphia: The Private Press Group of Philadelphia Graphic Arts Forum; 1939), p. 14.

103. Hugh Jones: *The Present State of Virginia (1724)* (New York: Reprinted for Joseph Sabin; 1865), pp. 87; 89.

104. "Proceedings of the Visitors of the William and Mary College, 1716," *The Virginia Magazine of History,* Vol. IV, (1896–97), p. 169.

105. *Virginia Gazette,* Nov. 18, 1737.

106. Quoted in R. E. Banta: *The Ohio* (New York: Rinehart & Company; 1949), p. 333.

107. Ann Hulton: *Letters of a Loyalist Lady* (Cambridge: Harvard University Press; 1927), p. 10.

108. *Pennsylvania Mercury* (Andrew Bradford), No. 181 (May 30, 1722).

109. Kenneth and Anna M. Roberts (trans.): *Moreau de St. Mery's American Journey (1793–1798)* (New York: Doubleday & Company; 1947), p. 333.

110. Ford, *op. cit.,* Vol. I, pp. 150, 149, 146.

111. Sylvia G. L. Dannett and Frank R. Rachel: *Down Memory Lane* (New York: Greenberg; 1954), p. 37.

112. *Connecticut Courant,* No. 1803 (Dec. 30, 1799).

113. Williams, *op. cit.,* p. 96.

114. *Virginia Gazette* (W. Parks), No. 480 (Oct. 10, 1745).

115. *Virginia Gazette* (W. Parks) No. 86 (Mar. 17, 1737); No. 87 (Mar. 24, 1738); No. 88 (Mar. 31, 1738).

116. *South Carolina Gazette.* Aug. 4, 1766; Nov. 17, 1766; Nov. 12, 1750. Quoted in Cohen, *op. cit., pp.* 82, 87.

117. *The Connecticut Courant.* No. 1792, May 29, 1799.

118. Roberts: *op. cit.,* pp. 290–91.

119. St. John De Crevecoeur; *Sketches of Eighteenth Century America.* Ed. by Henri L. Bourdin, Ralph Gabriel and T. Williams. (New Haven: Yale University Press; 1925), pp. 95–96.

120. *The Virginia Gazette* (W. Parks), No. 175 (Dec. 7, 1739).

121. Peter Cartwright: *Autobiography of Peter Cartwright.* Ed. by W. P. Strickland (New York: Carlton and Potter; 1857), pp. 25, 34.

122. Roberts: *op. cit.,* p. 60.

PART THREE

Dance Education in the Nineteenth Century

1. Cartwright, *op. cit.*, p. 75.

2. James Ford Rhodes: *History of the United States from the Compromise of 1850 to the McKinley-Bryant Campaign of 1896* (New York: The Macmillan Co.; 1920), Vol. II, pp. 63–64.

3. Caroline Cowles Richards: *Village Life in America, 1852–1872* (Henry Holt & Co.; 1913), pp. 128–29.

4. Samuel Miller: *Letters on Clerical Manners and Habits* (Princeton: Moore Baker; 1835), pp. 17–18, 32–33.

5. R. C. Galbraith Jr.: *The History of the Chillicothe Presbytery from the Organization in 1799–1889* (Chillicothe: By the Presbytery; 1889), pp. 22–23.

6. William E. Channing: "Address on Temperance; Delivered by request of the Council of Massachusetts Temperance Society at the Odeon, Boston, February 28, 1837," *The Works of William E. Channing, D.D.* (Boston: American Unitarian Association; 1896), pp. 110–11.

7. *The New York Times*, Feb. 18, 1894, p. 12, col. 1.

8. *The New York Times*, Dec. 17, 1897, p. 5, col. 4.

9. W. C. Wilkinson: *The Dance of Modern Society* (New York: Oakley, Mason & Co.; 1869), pp. 5, 24, 26.

10. *Ballou's Pictorial Drawing-Room Companion* (Boston), Vol. XI, Nov. 29, 1856, p. 349.

11. *Harpers New Monthly Magazine* (New York), Vol. LVI, April 1878, p. 785.

12. Able Bowen: *The Young Lady's Book*, 6th ed. (Boston: C. A. Wells; 1837). See also Arthur C. Cole: "The Puritan and Fair Terpsichore," *The Mississippi Valley Historical Review*, Vol. XXIX, No. 1 (June, 1942), for more about the champions of dance.

13. Mrs. John Sherwood: *Manners and Social Usages*, 4th ed. (New York: Harper & Brothers; 1887), p. 151.

14. Lyon G. Tyler: *The Letters and Times of the Tylers* (Richmond: Whittet & Shipperson; 1884), letter dated Dec. 26, 1827, to Mary Tyler, Vol. I, p. 390.

15. Mme. Celnart: *The Gentleman and Lady's Book of Politeness and Propriety of Deportment, Dedicated to the Youth of Both Sexes* (Boston: Allen and Ticknor; 1833), p. 187.

16. *Boston Weekly Magazine*, Vol. I, No. 47 (Aug. 30, 1817), p. 188.

17. Allen Dodworth: *Dancing and its Relation to Education and Social Life* (New York: Harper & Brothers; 1885), p. 62.

18. Allen Nevins and Milton Halsey Thomas (eds.): *The Diary of George Templeton Strong* (New York: The Macmillan Company; 1952), Vol. I, p. 270.

19. Mary Cosby Shelby: *Journal*. Ms. in the Samuel Wilson Collection, University of Kentucky Library, pp. 36–37.

20. Dodworth, *op. cit.*, pp. 15–16.

21. Francis Nichols; *A Guide to Politeness; or a System of Directions for the Aquirement of Ease, Propriety and Elegance of Manners* (Boston; Lincoln & Edmonds; 1810), p. 7.

22. T. S. Arthur: *Advice to Young Men on their Duties and Conduct in Life* (Boston: Phillips, Sampson & Co.; 1853), p. 69.

23. Anonymous: *Advice to Young Men, in a Series of Maxims Applying to All Classes, Particularly the Mercantile; or a Sure Guide to Gain Both Esteem and Estate* (Boston: Cummings, Hillard & Company, 1823), p. 62–63.

24. Daniel C. Eddy: *The Young Man's Friend* (Boston: Dayton and Wentworth; 1854), p. 112.

25. "The Economy of Literary and Religious Institutions," *American Journal of Education*, New Series, No. 1 (1830), p. 20.

26. *The Balance, and Columbian Respository* (Hudson, N.Y.), May 11, 1802.

27. F. Cuming: *Sketches of a Tour to the Western Country, 1807–1809*. In Ruben Gold Thwaite: *Early Western Travel* (Cleveland: The Arthur H. Clark Company; 1904), Vol. IV, pp. 188–89.

28. Nichols, *op. cit.*, pp. 5–6.

29. W. P. Hazard: *The Ball-Room Companion* (Philadelphia: George S. Appleton; 1894), p. 13.

30. Charles Durang: *The Ball-Room Bijou, and Art of Dancing* (Philadelphia: Fisher & Brother Co.; *ca.* 1855), p. 18.

31. D. L. Carpenter: *The Amateur's Preceptor on Dancing and Etiquette* (Philadelphia: M'Laughlin Brothers; 1854), p. 12.

32. E. Woodworth Masters: *The Standard Dance Album* (Boston: By the Author; 1883), p. iii.

33. Dodworth, *op. cit.*, pp. 11–12.

34. *Journal of Health* (Philadelphia), Vol. I (1830), p. 133.

35. Thomas Harris: *An Oration—Delivered Before the Philadelphia Medical Society* (Philadelphia: By the Society; 1831), p. 13.

36. J. C. Warren: *Importance of Physical Education* (Boston: Hillard Gray, Little & Wilkins; 1830), p. 20.

37. Charles Caldwell: *Thoughts on Physical Education* (Boston: Marsh, Capen & Lyons; 1834), pp. 64–65.

38. Ellwood P. Cubberly: *The History of Education* (Boston: Houghton Mifflin Company; 1920), Chap. XXVI.

39. *The Parents' Friend* (Philadelphia: B. Graves, 1803), Vol. II, Chap. 23.

40. Timothy Dwight: *Travels in New England and New York* (London: W. Baynes and Sons; 1823), Vol. II, p. 472.

41. Samuel G. Goodrich: *Peter Parley's Own Story* (New York: Sheldon & Company; 1846), p. 151.

42. Edward Everett Hale: *A New England Boyhood and other Bits of Autobiography: The Works of Edward Everett Hale* (Boston: Little, Brown & Company; 1905), Vol. VI, pp. 120–22.

43. *The Farmers' Almanack* (Robert B. Thomas), Dec., 1808.

44. John L. Blake: *The Farmer's Every-Day Book* (Auburn, N. H.: Derby, Miller Company; 1850), p. 165.

45. Salzman: *Gymnastics for Youth or a Practical Guide to Healthful and Amusing Exercises for the Use of Schools* (Philadelphia: William Duane, 1802), p. 331.

46. *The Centennial of the United States Military Academy at West Point, New York, 1802–1902* (Washington: Government Printing Office; 1904), Vol. I, p. 206.

47. William Arba Ellis (ed.): *Norwich University, 1819–1911.* (Montpelier, Vt.: The Capital City Press; 1911), Vol. I, pp. 10, 49, 55.

48. *American Journal of Education,* Vol. III (1828), p. 681.

49. *Hampshire Gazette,* (Northampton, Mass.), May 31, 1826.

50. Alma Lutz: *Emma Willard, Daughter of Democracy* (Boston: Houghton Mifflin; 1929), p. 37. The biographical material on Mrs. Willard is from Alma Lutz's book.

51. Emma Willard: *An Address to the Public; Particularly to the Members of the Legislature of New York, Proposing a Plan for the Improving of Female Education,* 2d ed. (Middlebury: J. W. Copeland; 1819), p. 38.

52. "Catherine Beecher," *Benard's American Journal of Education,* Vol. XXVIII (1878), p. 83.

53. Catherine Beecher: *A Treatise on Domestic Economy,* rev. ed. (New York: Harper & Brothers; 1854), p. 248.

54. Catherine Beecher: *Physiology and Calisthenics for School and Family* (New York: Harper & Brothers; 1856), p. 123.

55. *Ibid.,* p. 28.

56. Persis H. McCurdy: "The History of Physical Training at Mount Holyoke College," *American Physical Education Review,* Vol. XIV, March, 1909, p. 138.

57. *Calisthenic Exercises used at Mount Holyoke College* (n.p.; n.d.; *ca.* 1853). In Springfield College Library.

58. *Book of Duties.* In Mount Holyoke College Library.

59. *The Use of a Life: Memorials of Mrs. Z. P. Grant Banester* (New York: American Tract Society, 1885), p. 85.

60. Charles L. Coon: *North Carolina Schools and Academies, 1790–1840* (Raleigh: Edwards & Broughton Printing Co.; 1915), pp. 335–36.

61. Emma Lydia Balzau: *Almira Hart Lincoln Phelps, Her Life and Work* (Philadelphia: University of Pennsylvania; 1936), pp. 286–87.

62. J. E. Wendrow: "Collins D. Elliott and the Nashville Female Academy," *Tennessee Historical Magazine,* Series 2, Vol. III, No. 2 (Jan., 1935), pp. 82–86.

63. *The American Journal of Education,* Vol. X (June, 1861), p. 25.

64. William J. Akers: *Cleveland Schools in the Nineteenth Century* (Cleveland: W. M. Bayne Printing House; 1901), p. 35.

65. *Ibid.,* p. 80.

66. "Dancing in Cleveland High Schools," *The New York Times,* Dec. 30, 1894.

67. Francis W. Parker: *Talks on Pedagogics* (New York: E. L. Kellogg & Co.; 1894), pp. iv–v.

68. Mildred Spiesman: "American Pioneers in Educational Creative Dance," *Dance Magazine,* Nov., 1950, p. 35.

69. William H. S. Demarest: *A History of Rutgers College, 1766–1924* (New Brunswick: Rutgers College; 1924), p. 229.

70. Dorothy Lloyd Gilbert: *Guilford, A Quaker College* (Guilford College, N.C.: By Guilford College; 1937), pp. 131–32.

71. Edgar W. Knight (ed.): *A Documentary History of Education in the South Before 1860* (Chapel Hill: University of North Carolina Press; 1952), Vol. III, p. 283. See also pp. 369, 234.

72. Samuel Eliot Morison: *Three Centuries of Harvard, 1636–1936* (Cambridge: Harvard University Press; 1942), p. 208.

73. *The Analitic Magazine* (Philadelphia), Vol. 13 (1819), p. 114.

74 *American Journal of Education,* Vol. III (1928), p. 360.

75. Merton E. Coulter: *College Life in the Old South* (New York: The Macmillan Company; 1928), pp. 184–185.

76. Edwin L. Green: *History of the University of South Carolina* (Columbia: The State Company; 1916), p. 222.

77. Morison, *op. cit.*, p. 250.

78. Walter L. Fleming: *Louisiana State University, 1860–1896* (Baton Rouge: Louisiana State University; 1936), p. 459.

79. Dio Lewis: *The New Gymnastics for Men, Women and Children*, 6th ed. (Boston: Ticknor & Fields; 1864), p. 5.

80. *Ibid.*, p. 5.

81. Dio Lewis: *The Dio Lewis Treasury* (New York: The Canfield Publishing Company, 1887), pp. 625–26.

82. Fred E. Leonard and George B. Afflect: *A Guide to the History of Physical Education* (Philadelphia: Lea and Febiger; 1947), p. 266.

83. Harriet I. Ballintine: *The History of Physical Training at Vassar College* (Poughkeepsie: Lansing & Broas; 1915), p. 6.

84. Matthew Vassar: *Communications to the Board of Trustees of Vassar College* (New York: 1869), p. 45.

85. S. C. Staley and D. M. Lowery: *Manual of Gymnastic Dancing* (New York: Association Press; 1920), p. 9.

86. Ted Shawn: *Every Little Movement* (Pittsfield, Mass.: Eagle Printing & Binding Company; 1954), p. 15. See also Section IV for the influence of Delsarte on modern dance.

87. Genevieve Stebbins: *Delsarte System of Expression* (New York: Edgar S. Werner Publishing & Supply Co.; 1902), p. 400.

88. *Ibid.*, p. 401.

89. Emily M. Bishop: *Americanized Delsarte Culture* (Meadville: Flood and Vincent; 1892), p. 66.

90. William G. Anderson: *Light Gymnastics* (New York: Effingham, Maynard & Co., 1889), p. 183.

91. Leonard and Afflect, *op. cit.*, pp. 376–79.

92. Staley and Lowery, *op. cit.*, p. 14.

93. *Ibid.*, pp. 14–15.

94. Dumas Malone (ed.): *Dictionary of American Biography* (New York: Charles Scribner's Sons; 1935), Vol. XVI, pp. 355–56.

95. Staley and Lowery, *op. cit.,* p. 14.

96. Christian Eberhard: "Fancy Steps." In W. A. Strecher (ed.): *A Text-Book of German-American System of Gymnastics* (Boston: Lea & Shephard; 1895), Chap. 9.

97. Program for Visitor's Day, Summer School of Physical Training, Hemenway Gymnasium, Harvard University, Cambridge, Mass., Aug. 4, 1892. In Springfield College Library.

98. Melvin Ballou Gilbert (edited by Susan H. Gilman): *Gilbert Dances* (New York: G. Schirmer, 1913), Vol. I, p. 1.

99. Melvin Ballou Gilbert: "Classic Dancing," *American Physical Education Review,* Vol. X (June, 1905), p. 153.

100. Dudley A. Sargent: "Dancing Useful from the Standpoint of Physical Training," *Mind and Body,* Vol. XVI (Oct., 1909), p. 220.

101. *Harvard University Announcement of Summer Courses of Instruction* (1894), p. 27.

102. Carl L. Schrader: "The Old Hemenway Gymnasium," *Journal of Health and Physical Education,* Sept., 1948, p. 477.

103. Staley and Lowery, *op. cit.,* p. 17.

104. Quoted in Henry James: *Charles W. Eliot, President of Harvard University, 1869–1909* (Boston: Houghton Mifflin Company; 1930), Vol. II, p. 163.

Index